Yorkshire Travel Guide 2023

The Updated Pocket Guide Packed with Insider Tips, Local Secrets, and everything you need to know for a perfect trip to this England Historic county

Charles J. Norris

Copyright 2023 by Charles J. Norris. All rights reserved. No part of this publication may be reproduced, distributed, or transmitted in any form or by any means, including photocopying, recording, or other electronic or mechanical methods, without the prior written permission of the publisher, except in the case of brief quotations embodied in critical reviews and certain other noncommercial uses permitted by copyright law.

Table of Contents

Table of Contents..2
My Yorkshire Story.. 6
Introduction... 8
1. Welcome to Yorkshire: A Brief Overview... 10
27 Best things to do in Yorkshire...................13
2. Getting to Yorkshire.................................... 16
    2.1. By Air..16
    2.2. By Train... 17
    2.3. By Car... 17
    2.4. By Bus...18
    Which option is right for you?..................... 18
3. Yorkshire Essential Information............... 20
    3.1. Currency and Exchange...................... 20
    3.2. Language and Communication........... 22
    3.3. Time Zone... 25
    3.4. Weather and Climate...........................26
4. Yorkshire at a Glance..................................29
    4.1. Geographical Overview....................... 29
    4.2. History and Heritage........................... 30
    4.3. Culture and Traditions........................ 33
5. Exploring Yorkshire.................................... 36
    5.1. Yorkshire Dales...................................36

    5.1.1. The North Yorkshire Moors..36
    5.1.2. The Yorkshire Wolds............37
    5.1.3. Yorkshire Dales National Park.. 37

  5.2. Historic Cities and Towns..................39
    5.2.1. York...............................39
    5.2.2. Leeds............. 43
    5.2.3. Sheffield............... 48
    5.2.4. Bradford............... 51

  5.3. Coastal Escapes...............................54
  5.3.1. Whitby................................54
  5.3.2. Scarborough........................ 58
  5.3.3. Filey................. 62

  5.4. Rural Retreats..................................65
  5.4.1. Haworth................................65
  5.4.2. Ripon..................................68
  5.4.3. Harrogate............................71

6. Planning Your Trip To Yorkshire.............75
  6.1. Best Time to Visit.............................. 75
  6.2. Duration of Stay................................77
  6.3. Accommodation Options.................... 79
  6.4. Transportation within Yorkshire......... 82

7. Top Attractions and Landmarks in Yorkshire... 85
  7.1. York Minster....................................... 85
  7.2. The Yorkshire Sculpture Park............. 89

7.3. Fountains Abbey and Studley Royal Water Garden.. 92
7.4. Bolton Abbey.. 98
7.5. Whitby Abbey.................................... 102
7.6. Harewood House............................... 107
7.7. Castle Howard................................... 111

8. Outdoor Activities and Adventure in Yorkshire.. 115
8.1. Hiking and Walking Trails................ 115
8.2. Cycling Routes.................................. 118
8.3. Water Sports and Sailing.................. 122
8.4. Wildlife and Nature Reserves........... 127

9. Immersing in Yorkshire's Culinary Delights.. 130
9.1. Traditional Yorkshire Dishes............ 130
9.2. Local Breweries and Pubs................. 133
9.3. Farmers' Markets and Food Festivals..... 136

10. Shopping in Yorkshire........................... 141
10.1. Independent Boutiques and Shops.. 141
10.2. Antique and Vintage Stores............ 145
10.3. Artisan Crafts and Souvenirs.......... 149

11. Insider Tips and Local Secrets.............. 152
11.1. Hidden Gems and Lesser-known Attractions... 152
11.2. Authentic Local Experiences.......... 154

12. Practical Information and Resources.. 158
   12.1. Tourist Information Centers............ 158
   12.2. Emergency Contacts....................... 160
   12.3. Health and Safety............................ 161
   12.4. Useful Websites and Apps.............. 162

13. Conclusion: Making the Most of Your Yorkshire Adventure................................... 165
   13.1. Reflecting on Your Journey............ 165
   13.2. Creating Lasting Memories.............166
   13.3. Farewell to Yorkshire...................... 166

My Yorkshire Story

As I stepped foot in the captivating county of Yorkshire, little did I know that I was about to embark on a deeply emotional journey. The moment I set eyes on the magnificent ruins of Whitby Abbey, standing majestically on the cliffs, a wave of nostalgia washed over me. Memories of childhood stories flooded my mind, evoking a profound sense of connection to the past.

Wandering through the historic streets of York, I found myself drawn to the ancient walls that whispered tales of battles fought and lost. The weight of history enveloped me, and I couldn't help but feel a deep appreciation for those who came before, shaping the very fabric of this remarkable place.

But it was in the remote Yorkshire Dales where my emotions truly soared. As I hiked along the verdant hills, surrounded by breathtaking landscapes, I couldn't help but be overwhelmed by a profound sense of awe and tranquility. The untouched beauty of nature reminded me of the fragile yet resilient nature of life itself.

Yorkshire had become more than just a destination; it had become a tapestry of emotions woven into my heart. It awakened a longing to embrace the beauty of the world, to cherish the fleeting moments that make life truly meaningful.

In the end, Yorkshire had gifted me not only with remarkable sights but also with a renewed sense of purpose and a deeper appreciation for the power of connection, history, and nature. It had touched my soul in ways I never expected, leaving an indelible mark on my journey through life.

Introduction

Nestled in the heart of England, Yorkshire beckons travelers with its idyllic countryside, dramatic coastlines, and enchanting towns steeped in history. Whether you're a nature lover, a history enthusiast, a foodie seeking culinary delights, or simply a curious explorer, Yorkshire has something extraordinary to offer.

This comprehensive travel guide is meticulously crafted to be your trusted companion, ensuring that you make the most of your Yorkshire experience. Discover hidden gems and local secrets, navigate the winding streets of historic cities, and immerse yourself in the breathtaking beauty of the Yorkshire Dales.

Uncover the stories that shaped this remarkable county, from ancient ruins and majestic castles to quaint villages and bustling market towns. Engage with the warmth and hospitality of the locals, who are eager to share their traditions, legends, and insider knowledge with you.

Whether you're planning a weekend getaway or a longer expedition, this guide will provide you with invaluable insights, practical tips, and a wealth of information to help you create unforgettable memories. From planning your itinerary to exploring top attractions, indulging in local cuisine, and venturing off the beaten path, every aspect of your Yorkshire adventure is covered.

So, grab your copy of the "Yorkshire Travel Guide 2023" and let the pages transport you to a world where picturesque landscapes, captivating history, and genuine hospitality await. Get ready to fall in love with Yorkshire as you uncover its hidden treasures and embrace the magic that awaits around every corner. The options are boundless, and your journey begins right here.

1. Welcome to Yorkshire: A Brief Overview

The largest county in the UK by area is Yorkshire, which is located in Northern England. It has some of England's most stunning countryside as well as a rich history and culture.

Yorkshire is divided into three administrative counties: the East Riding, the North Riding, and the West Riding. The city of York is also a separate administrative unit.

The county is known for its moorland, dales, and coastline. The North York Moors and Yorkshire Dales National Parks are both located in Yorkshire, as is part of the Peak District National Park. Nidderdale and the Howardian Hills are designated Areas of Outstanding Natural Beauty.

Yorkshire is also home to a number of famous cities and towns, including Leeds, Sheffield, Kingston upon Hull, Bradford, and Wakefield. These cities are all major economic and cultural centers, and they offer a wide range of attractions for visitors.

Some of the most popular tourist destinations in Yorkshire include:

The Yorkshire Dales National Park, a UNESCO World Heritage Site; York Minster, the biggest Gothic church in Northern Europe. Area of Outstanding Natural Beauty designation for the North York Moors National Park.
  Filey, a well-known beach resort; Whitby, a historic coastal town with a magnificent port.
  Scarborough, a historic seaside community.
  Sheffield, a significant industrial city with a lively arts community.
  Leeds, a significant financial and commercial hub.

Yorkshire is a beautiful and diverse county with something to offer everyone. Whether you're interested in history, culture, nature, or simply a relaxing break, Yorkshire is the perfect place to visit.

Here are some additional facts about Yorkshire:

The name "Yorkshire" comes from the Old English words "Eoforwicscire", meaning "the shire of the people of Eoforwic".

The county was originally divided into three ridings: the East Riding, the North Riding, and the West Riding.

Yorkshire was a major center of the Industrial Revolution, and its cities and towns played a key role in the development of the textile, steel, and coal industries.

Yorkshire is home to a number of famous people, including the Brontë sisters, Harold Wilson, and David Hockney.

The Yorkshire Terrier, a popular breed of dog, is named after the county.

27 Best things to do in Yorkshire

Visit York Minster, one of the largest Gothic cathedrals in Northern Europe.

Explore the city of York, a UNESCO World Heritage Site.

Go on a day trip to the Yorkshire Dales National Park, a beautiful area of rolling hills, valleys, and waterfalls.

Visit the Brontë Parsonage Museum in Haworth, where the Brontë sisters lived and wrote their famous novels.

Hike up Pen-y-ghent, the highest peak in the Yorkshire Dales.

Visit the Eden Camp Museum, a former prisoner-of-war camp that has been converted into a museum about World War II.

Go on a steam train ride on the North Yorkshire Moors Railway.

Visit the Royal Armouries Museum in Leeds, home to a vast collection of arms and armor from around the world.

See a show at the Grand Theatre in Leeds, one of the largest theaters in the UK.

Visit the Hepworth Wakefield, a modern art gallery with a collection of works by Henry Moore and other British artists.

Go shopping in the historic market town of Skipton.

Visit the National Railway Museum in York, home to a collection of over 100 locomotives and rolling stock.

Go on a boat trip on the River Ouse in York.

Visit the Yorkshire Sculpture Park, a sculpture park in West Bretton with over 200 works of art.

Hike the Three Peaks, a challenging walk that takes in the peaks of Pen-y-ghent, Whernside, and Ingleborough.

Visit the Robin Hood's Bay, a picturesque fishing village on the North Sea coast.

Go on a ghost walk in York, a city with a rich history of hauntings.

Visit the Masham Brewery, one of the oldest breweries in England.

Sample some of Yorkshire's famous pies, such as a Melton Mowbray pork pie or a Wensleydale cheese pie.

Visit the National Trust's Fountains Abbey and Studley Royal Water Gardens, a beautiful 18th-century estate with stunning gardens and a ruined abbey.

Go stargazing in the Yorkshire Dales, one of the darkest areas in England.

Visit the National Coal Mining Museum for England in Wakefield, a former coal mine that has been converted into a museum.

Go on a safari at Flamingo Land Theme Park in North Yorkshire.

Visit the Yorkshire Air Museum in Elvington, home to a collection of aircraft from World War II and the Cold War.

Go on a day trip to Whitby, a charming seaside town with a rich history.

Visit the Saltaire Village, a UNESCO World Heritage Site that was built by Sir Titus Salt in the 19th century.

2. Getting to Yorkshire

2.1. By Air

There are two major airports in Yorkshire: Leeds Bradford Airport (LBA) and Robin Hood Airport Doncaster Sheffield (DSA). LBA is the larger of the two airports, and it is served by a wider range of airlines. DSA is a smaller airport, but it is located closer to some of the most popular tourist destinations in Yorkshire, such as Sheffield and Doncaster.

Flights from London to LBA or DSA typically take around an hour. There are also direct flights to Yorkshire from other major cities in the UK, such as Manchester, Birmingham, and Edinburgh.

2.2. By Train

Yorkshire is well-served by the National Rail network. There are direct trains from London to Leeds, York, Sheffield, and many other towns and cities in the county. The journey time from London to Leeds is around two hours, and the journey time from London to York is around two and a half hours.

2.3. By Car

Yorkshire is easily accessible by car. The M1 motorway runs through the county, and there are a number of other major roads that connect Yorkshire to other parts of the UK. The journey time from London to Yorkshire by car is around four hours.

2.4. By Bus

There are a number of bus companies that operate services to Yorkshire. The National Express is the largest bus company in the UK, and it operates services to all major towns and cities in Yorkshire. There are also a number of smaller bus companies that operate services to more rural areas of the county.

The journey time from London to Yorkshire by bus is around five hours.

Which option is right for you?

The best way to get to Yorkshire depends on your individual needs and preferences. If you are on a tight budget, then bus travel may be the best option for you. If you are traveling from a major city in the UK, then train travel may be the most convenient option. And if you are traveling from abroad, then flying may be the best way to get to Yorkshire.

No matter which option you choose, you are sure to have a great time exploring Yorkshire. The county has something to offer everyone, from stunning countryside to historic cities. So what are you waiting for? Start planning your trip today.

3. Yorkshire Essential Information

3.1. Currency and Exchange

The currency of Yorkshire is the pound sterling (GBP). The exchange rate for the pound sterling as of today (21/06/2023) is:

1 GBP = 1.20 USD
1 GBP = 1.12 EUR
1 GBP = 147.79 INR

There are many places to exchange currency in Yorkshire, including banks, currency exchange bureaus, and online providers. When exchanging currency, it is important to shop around and compare rates to get the best deal.

Here are some of the best places to exchange currency in Yorkshire:

No1 Currency Exchange has a number of branches in Yorkshire, and they offer competitive exchange rates.

Thomas Exchange Global is another good option for exchanging currency in Yorkshire. They have a wide range of currencies available, and their rates are competitive.

Travelex is a well-known currency exchange brand, and they have a number of branches in Yorkshire. Their rates are generally competitive, but they may charge a commission.

If you are looking to exchange currency online, there are a number of reputable providers that offer competitive rates. Some of the best include:

XE
TransferWise
OFX

When exchanging currency online, it is important to read the terms and conditions carefully to ensure that you understand the fees that will be charged.

Here are some tips for exchanging currency in Yorkshire:

Shop around and compare rates before you exchange currency.
Consider using an online provider to get the best deal.
Be aware of the fees that will be charged.
Only exchange the amount of currency that you need.
Keep your exchange receipt in case you need to make a claim.

3.2. Language and Communication

The language and communication in Yorkshire is a complex and fascinating topic. There are many different dialects of Yorkshire English, each with its own unique features. Some of the most common features of Yorkshire English include:

The use of the "th" sound as a "t" sound, as in "t'other" for "the other".

The use of the "wh" sound as a "w" sound, as in "whur" for "where".

The use of the "a" sound as an "o" sound, as in "cawd" for "caught".

The use of the "eh" sound as a question tag, as in "that's a nice dog, eh?".

In addition to these phonological features, there are also many lexical differences between Yorkshire English and other varieties of English. For example, in Yorkshire English, the word "bairn" is used for "child", "hap" is used for "happen", and "scran" is used for "food".

The use of Yorkshire English can vary depending on the speaker's age, social class, and region. For example, younger speakers are more likely to use standard English features, while older speakers are more likely to use traditional Yorkshire features. Similarly, people from different regions of Yorkshire may use different words or pronunciations.

Despite these variations, there is a strong sense of identity associated with Yorkshire English. Many people in Yorkshire are proud of their dialect and see it as a way of expressing their regional identity. As a result, Yorkshire English is still widely used in the region, even though it is not the official language of England.

Here are some examples of Yorkshire English phrases:

"I'm reet ganny" - I'm really going.
"A'm oop fort" - I'm up for it.
"Tha's reet canny" - That's really good.
"Tha's nowt but a load o' cobblers" - That's nothing but nonsense.
"A'll see thee reet" - I'll see you later.

If you are interested in learning more about Yorkshire English, there are many resources available online and in libraries. You can also find Yorkshire English courses offered by some universities and colleges.

3.3. Time Zone

Yorkshire is in the GMT+1 time zone, also known as British Summer Time (BST). This means that Yorkshire is 1 hour ahead of Coordinated Universal Time (UTC). During the winter months, when daylight saving time is not in effect, Yorkshire is in the GMT time zone.

The current time in Yorkshire is 2023-06-21 14:39:56 BST. If you are in a different time zone, you can use a time zone converter to find out what time it is in Yorkshire.

Here are some other countries that are in the same time zone as Yorkshire:

Belgium
Denmark
France
Germany
Ireland
Netherlands
Norway

Sweden

If you are traveling to Yorkshire from a country that is in a different time zone, be sure to adjust your watch accordingly. For example, if you are traveling from the United States, which is in the UTC-4 time zone, you will need to add 5 hours to your watch when you arrive in Yorkshire.

3.4. Weather and Climate

Yorkshire has a maritime climate, which means that it is influenced by the Atlantic Ocean. This means that the summers are typically warm rather than hot, and the winters are cool to cold. The average temperature in July and August is around 20°C, while the average temperature in January is around 4°C.

Yorkshire does get snow, but the amount of snow that falls varies from year to year. North Yorkshire in particular is an area which usually receives a large amount of snowfall. Areas such as Harrogate and Skipton are almost always affected by cold-weather fronts.

The wettest months in Yorkshire are October, November, and December. The driest months are April, May, and June. The average annual rainfall in Yorkshire is around 750mm.

The weather in Yorkshire can be unpredictable, so it is always a good idea to check the forecast before you travel. However, if you are looking for a region with a variety of weather conditions, Yorkshire is a good choice.

Here is a table of the average monthly temperatures and rainfall in Yorkshire:

	A	B	C
1	Month	Temperature (°C)	Rainfall (mm)
2	January	4	55
3	February	6	45
4	March	9	40
5	April	12	35
6	May	15	30
7	June	18	25
8	July	20	20
9	August	20	20
10	September	17	25
11	October	14	30
12	November	10	40
13	December	7	50

4. Yorkshire at a Glance

4.1. Geographical Overview

Yorkshire is the largest county in England by area, and is home to a diverse range of landscapes, from the high Pennine moorlands to the North York Moors and the Yorkshire Wolds.

The geographical overview of Yorkshire can be divided into four broad belts:

The Pennine moorlands: These moorlands stretch across the western part of Yorkshire, and are home to some of the highest peaks in England, including Pen-y-ghent (2,273 feet) and Whernside (2,415 feet).
The Yorkshire Dales: These dales are a series of valleys that cut through the Pennine moorlands. They are known for their picturesque scenery, including rolling hills, waterfalls, and limestone caves.

The Vale of York: This lowland area lies in the central part of Yorkshire. It is drained by the River Ouse, and is home to the cities of York, Leeds, and Sheffield.

The North York Moors and Yorkshire Wolds: These two areas lie in the eastern part of Yorkshire. The North York Moors are a national park, and are known for their heather moorland, forests, and dramatic coastline. The Yorkshire Wolds are a chalk upland, and are known for their rolling hills, windmills, and villages.

In addition to these four belts, Yorkshire also includes the Humber Estuary, which is the largest estuary in England. The Humber Estuary is home to a variety of wildlife, including seals, dolphins, and seabirds.

4.2. History and Heritage

Yorkshire has a rich and diverse history that dates back thousands of years. The region was first occupied by humans after the retreat of the ice age, and has been home to a variety of cultures and civilizations over the centuries.

Some of the earliest evidence of human occupation in Yorkshire comes from the Mesolithic period (around 10,000-5,000 BC). During this time, hunter-gatherers lived in the region, and their remains have been found at sites such as Star Carr, near Scarborough.

In the Iron Age (around 800-43 BC), Yorkshire was inhabited by the Brigantes, a Celtic tribe. The Brigantes were a powerful force in the region, and their territory stretched from the Humber to the Tees.

The Romans invaded Yorkshire in AD 71, and the Brigantes were eventually defeated. The Romans ruled Yorkshire for over 300 years, and they left a lasting legacy in the form of roads, towns, and fortifications.

After the fall of the Roman Empire, Yorkshire was ruled by a variety of different peoples, including the Angles, Saxons, and Vikings. The

Vikings were particularly influential in Yorkshire, and they left their mark on the region's language, culture, and place names.

In the 11th century, Yorkshire was conquered by the Normans. The Normans built many castles in Yorkshire, and they also established the city of York as a major center of trade and commerce.

Yorkshire played an important role in the English Civil War (1642-1651). The county was divided between Royalists and Parliamentarians, and there were many battles fought in Yorkshire during the war.

In the 18th and 19th centuries, Yorkshire was at the forefront of the Industrial Revolution. The county's coalfields and ironworks helped to fuel the Industrial Revolution, and Yorkshire became a major center of industry.

Today, Yorkshire is a vibrant and diverse region with a rich history. The county is home to a variety of historical sites, including castles, abbeys, and museums. Yorkshire is also a popular tourist destination, and visitors can enjoy the region's stunning countryside, historic cities, and world-class food and drink.

4.3. Culture and Traditions

Here are some of the most famous cultural traditions of Yorkshire:

The Yorkshire Pudding: This savory pancake is a staple of Sunday roast dinners in Yorkshire. It is traditionally cooked in the drippings from the roast meat, which gives it a delicious flavor.

The Dales: The Yorkshire Dales are a beautiful region of rolling hills, valleys, and rivers. They are a popular destination for hiking, camping, and fishing.

The Brontë Sisters: The Brontë sisters, Charlotte, Emily, and Anne, were all born in Yorkshire. They are famous for their novels, which often explore themes of love, loss, and the power of nature.

The Yorkshire Dales National Park: The Yorkshire Dales National Park is one of the most popular national parks in England. It is home to a variety of wildlife, including deer, foxes, and grouse.

The Yorkshire Terrier: The Yorkshire Terrier is a small, long-haired dog that is native to Yorkshire. They are known for their friendly and playful nature.

The White Rose of York: The White Rose of York is a symbol of Yorkshire. It was used by the House of York during the Wars of the Roses.

Here are some other cultural traditions of Yorkshire that are worth mentioning:

The Long Sword Dance: This traditional dance is performed by a group of men who carry long swords. It is thought to have originated in the 17th century.

On Ilkla Moor Baht 'at: This song is considered to be the unofficial anthem of Yorkshire. It was written in the 19th century and tells the story of a man who is lost on Ilkley Moor.

Yorkshire Day: This annual holiday is celebrated on 1 August. It is a day to celebrate all things Yorkshire, from its culture and history to its food and drink.

5. Exploring Yorkshire

5.1. Yorkshire Dales

The Yorkshire Dales is a region of outstanding natural beauty in the north of England. It is home to some of the most dramatic scenery in the country, including towering mountains, deep valleys, and winding rivers. The area is also rich in history and culture, with many ancient villages and towns to explore.

5.1.1. The North Yorkshire Moors

The North Yorkshire Moors is a designated Area of Outstanding Natural Beauty (AONB) in North Yorkshire, England. It is a popular tourist destination, known for its dramatic scenery, including rolling hills, moorland, and dramatic cliffs. The area is also home to a number of historic villages and towns, including Whitby, Helmsley, and Pickering.

5.1.2. The Yorkshire Wolds

The Yorkshire Wolds is a chalk upland in North Yorkshire, England. It is a designated AONB, and is known for its rolling hills, lush meadows, and historic villages. The area is also home to a number of important archaeological sites, including the Neolithic settlement of Star Carr.

5.1.3. Yorkshire Dales National Park

The Yorkshire Dales National Park is a national park in North Yorkshire, England. It is the largest national park in the North of England, and is home to some of the most spectacular scenery in the country. The park is a popular destination for hiking, camping, and fishing. It is also home to a number of historic villages and towns, including Hawes, Settle, and Malham.

Some of the things you can do in the Yorkshire Dales include:

Hiking: There are a number of well-marked hiking trails in the Yorkshire Dales, ranging from easy walks to challenging treks.

Camping: There are a number of campsites in the Yorkshire Dales, where you can pitch your tent and enjoy the great outdoors.

Fishing: The Yorkshire Dales is home to a number of rivers and lakes, where you can fish for trout, salmon, and other species.

Visiting historic villages and towns: The Yorkshire Dales is home to a number of historic villages and towns, each with its own unique charm.

Exploring the local wildlife: The Yorkshire Dales is home to a variety of wildlife, including red squirrels, badgers, and kingfishers.

Enjoying the scenery: The Yorkshire Dales is simply stunning, and there are few better places to enjoy the beauty of the English countryside.

If you are planning a trip to the Yorkshire Dales, here are some tips:

Go when it's pleasant outside and less crowded, such as in the spring or fall.

Be sure to pack plenty of walking shoes, sunscreen, and a hat.

If you are planning on camping, be sure to book your campsite in advance.

Explore the local villages and towns, and learn about the area's history and culture.

Take some time to enjoy the scenery, and soak up the beauty of the Yorkshire Dales.

5.2. Historic Cities and Towns

5.2.1. York

York is a historic city in North Yorkshire, England. It is the county town of the county of York and the historic county of Yorkshire. York is a UNESCO World Heritage Site and is one of the most visited cities in the United Kingdom.

The history of the city dates back to the Roman era and is lengthy and rich. York was originally known as Eboracum when it was established by the Romans in 71 AD. The city served as a significant Roman commerce and military hub. York was ruled by the Anglo-Saxons in the fifth century, after the Romans left Britain. York served as the Northumbria Kingdom's capital during the ninth century.

In the Middle Ages, York played a significant role in the wool trade. Numerous places of worship were also located in the city, including the York Minster, one of Europe's biggest Gothic cathedrals.

Both in 1314 and 1644, during the English Civil War, the Scots besieged York. During World War II, the city also sustained significant bombing.

Today, York is a thriving city with a population of over 200,000 people. The city is a popular tourist destination, thanks to its rich history, its many historical buildings, and its vibrant cultural scene.

Some of the must-see attractions in York include:

The Minster of York: This is one of the largest Gothic cathedrals in Europe. It was founded in the 7th century and has been rebuilt several times over the centuries. The Minster is a UNESCO World Heritage Site and is one of the most popular tourist attractions in York.

The Shambles: This is a narrow, winding street in the heart of York. It is lined with medieval shops and restaurants. The Shambles is one of the most photographed streets in York.

York Castle: This is a Norman castle that was built in the 11th century. The castle is now a museum and is home to a number of historical exhibits.

Clifford's Tower: This is a ruined medieval castle that is located on a hill overlooking the city. The tower was built in the 12th century and was used as a prison until the 18th century.

Jorvik Viking Centre: This is a museum that tells the story of the Vikings in York. The museum is located in a reconstructed Viking village.

National Railway Museum: This is a museum that tells the story of the railways in Britain. The museum is located in York and is one of the largest railway museums in the world.

In addition to the historical attractions, York also has a number of other things to offer visitors, including:

A vibrant cultural scene: York has a number of theaters, art galleries, and museums. The city also hosts a number of festivals throughout the year, including the York Mystery Plays, which are a series of medieval plays that are performed every year in July and August. ·

A wide variety of shops and restaurants: York has a wide variety of shops and restaurants to choose from. The city has a number of independent shops, as well as chain stores.

There are also a number of restaurants serving food from all over the world.

A number of green spaces: York has a number of green spaces, including the River Ouse, which runs through the city, and the York Walls, which offer stunning views of the city.

York is a great place to visit for a weekend or a longer stay. There is something for everyone in this historic city.

5.2.2. Leeds

West Yorkshire is the home of Leeds, an English city. After London and Birmingham, it is the third-largest city in the United Kingdom. Leeds serves as a significant hub for business, industry, and education. One of the biggest universities in the UK, the University of Leeds, is located there. Leeds is a well-liked travel location as well. In Leeds, a few of the most well-liked tourist attractions are:

The Royal Armouries: is a museum dedicated to weapons and armor. One of the world's biggest museums of its sort, it. The Royal Armouries collection includes over 8,500 objects, dating from the 11th century to the present day. The museum is divided into four main sections: the Medieval, the Renaissance, the 18th Century, and the 20th Century. The Medieval section includes suits of armor worn by knights in the Middle Ages. The Renaissance section includes armor worn by knights and soldiers during the Renaissance. The 18th Century section includes firearms and swords from the 18th century. The 20th Century section includes weapons from World War I and World War II.

The Leeds City Museum: is a museum of the history of Leeds. The museum's collection includes objects from the city's past, including Roman artifacts, medieval weapons, and industrial machinery. The museum is divided into four main sections: the Archaeology, the History, the Industry, and the People. The Archaeology section includes objects from the city's Roman and medieval past. The History section includes objects from the city's industrial past. The Industry section includes objects from the city's textile and engineering industries. The People section includes objects from the city's social history.

The Hepworth Wakefield: is a gallery of modern and contemporary art. The gallery's collection includes works by Pablo Picasso, Henry Moore, and Damien Hirst. The gallery is housed in a striking building designed by David Chipperfield. The gallery has a number of permanent exhibitions, as well as temporary exhibitions that change regularly.

The Leeds Town Hall: is a Grade I listed building. It is the seat of Leeds City Council. The town hall was built in the 19th century and is a fine example of Victorian architecture. The town hall is open to the public for tours.

The Leeds Art Gallery: is a gallery of fine art. The gallery's collection includes works by Rembrandt, Van Gogh, and Monet. The gallery is housed in a beautiful building in the city center. The gallery has a number of permanent exhibitions, as well as temporary exhibitions that change regularly.

Leeds Castle: is a moated castle. It is located just outside of Leeds city center. The castle was built in the 12th century and has been the home of several English noble families. The castle is open to the public for tours.

The Leeds Minster: is a cathedral. It is the seat of the Diocese of Leeds. The minster was built in the 13th century and is a fine example of Gothic architecture. The minster is open to the public for worship and for tours.

The Leeds Markets: are a series of covered markets. They are located in the heart of Leeds city center. The markets sell a wide variety of goods, including food, clothing, and souvenirs. The markets are open seven days a week.

There is a professional football team called Leeds United. In England's top division of football, the Premier League, the club competes. Having won the league title three times and the FA Cup twice, Leeds United is one of the most successful teams in English football history. Elland Road is where the club is based.

The cultural scene of Leeds is thriving in addition to these other attractions. Theaters, movie theaters, and music venues can be found around the city. With many businesses to select from, Leeds is also a well-liked shopping location.

Leeds is a great city to visit for a weekend break or a longer vacation. There is something for everyone in Leeds, from history and culture lovers to shoppers and sports fans.

Here are some additional tips for planning your trip to Leeds:

Leeds is most pleasant in the spring or fall, when temperatures are moderate.
If you are interested in history and culture, be sure to visit the Royal Armouries, the Leeds City Museum, and the Hepworth Wakefield.
If you are a shopper, be sure to visit the Leeds Markets and the Headrow.
If you are a sports fan, be sure to catch a Leeds United football match at Elland Road.
Leeds is a relatively affordable city to visit.

5.2.3. Sheffield

In the English county of South Yorkshire, the city of Sheffield is located. With a population of more than 575,000, it is the fifth-largest city in England. The steel industry in Sheffield, which formerly dominated the globe, is well recognized. The city's economy has, however, changed in recent years, and it is now a significant hub for commerce, instruction, and culture.

Sheffield is a beautiful city with a lot to offer visitors. The city center is home to many historical buildings, including Sheffield Cathedral, the Town Hall, and the Millennium Gallery. There are also a number of museums in Sheffield, such as the National Videogame Museum, the Sheffield Industrial Museum, and the Kelham Island Museum.

If you enjoy outdoor activities, Sheffield is the perfect place for you. The city is surrounded by hills and forests, and there are a number of parks and trails to explore. You can go hiking, biking, or fishing in the Peak District National Park, which is just a short drive from Sheffield.

Sheffield is also a great place to visit for its nightlife. The city has a vibrant bar and club scene, and there are always something going on. If you're looking for a more traditional English experience, you can visit one of the many pubs in Sheffield.

Here are a few of Sheffield's major attractions:

Visit Sheffield Cathedral: This beautiful cathedral is the oldest building in Sheffield and is a Grade I listed building.
Explore the city center: The city center is home to many historical buildings, as well as a number of shops, restaurants, and bars.
Visit the Millennium Gallery: This gallery houses a collection of modern and contemporary art.

Go shopping: Sheffield has a great selection of shops, from high-street chains to independent boutiques.

Visit the National Videogame Museum: This museum is dedicated to the history of video games.

Go hiking or biking in the Peak District National Park: This national park is just a short drive from Sheffield and offers stunning views of the surrounding countryside.

Visit one of the many pubs in Sheffield: Sheffield has a great selection of pubs, so you're sure to find one that suits your taste.

If you're looking for a city with a lot to offer, Sheffield is the perfect place for you. With its history, culture, and natural beauty, Sheffield is sure to impress.

Here are some additional tips for planning your trip to Sheffield:

The best time to visit Sheffield is during the spring or fall, when the weather is mild.

If you're planning on doing any hiking or biking, be sure to pack appropriate clothing and footwear.

If you're interested in visiting the Peak District National Park, be sure to purchase a National Park Pass.

Sheffield is a relatively affordable city, so you won't have to break the bank to enjoy your trip.

5.2.4. Bradford

Bradford is a city in West Yorkshire, England. It is the fifth-largest city in Yorkshire, and the 12th-largest city in England. Bradford is a major center for industry and commerce, and is home to the headquarters of many major companies, including Marks & Spencer and Tetley Tea.

Bradford is also a city with a rich history and culture. It is home to many historical buildings, including Bradford Cathedral, the National Media Museum, and the Bradford Industrial

Museum. The city is also home to a number of museums and art galleries, as well as a vibrant theater scene.

Bradford Cathedral is a Grade I listed building that was built in the 19th century. The cathedral is a beautiful example of Gothic Revival architecture, and is one of the most popular tourist attractions in Bradford.

The National Media Museum is a museum dedicated to the history of film, television, and photography. The museum is home to a collection of over 3 million objects, including film posters, scripts, costumes, and props. The museum also has a number of interactive exhibits that allow visitors to learn about the history of media.

The Bradford Industrial Museum is a museum that tells the story of the industrial history of Bradford. The museum is home to a collection of over 20,000 objects, including machinery, tools, and textiles. The museum also has a number of interactive exhibits that allow visitors to learn about the history of industry in Bradford.

In addition to its historical and cultural attractions, Bradford is also a vibrant and exciting city with something to offer everyone. The city has a thriving shopping scene, with a number of large shopping malls and independent stores. Bradford is also home to a number of excellent restaurants, bars, and clubs.

Bradford is a great place to visit for a weekend break or a longer vacation. The city has something to offer everyone, from history lovers to culture vultures to shoppers. If you are looking for a city with a rich history, a vibrant culture, and plenty of things to do, then Bradford is the perfect place for you.

Here are some other things to do in Bradford:

Visit the Alhambra Theatre, one of the oldest and largest theaters in the UK.

Go shopping in the city's many markets, including the Bradford Wool Exchange and the Kirkgate Market.

Take a walk through Bradford's parks and gardens, including Lister Park and Bradford City Park.

Visit the Bradford City Hall, a beautiful example of Victorian architecture.

Sample the local cuisine, which includes a variety of Indian, Pakistani, and Bangladeshi dishes.

5.3. Coastal Escapes

5.3.1. Whitby

Whitby is a town on the North Sea coast of Yorkshire, England. It is a popular tourist destination, known for its abbey, its narrow streets, and its fishing industry. The town is also home to the Whitby Goth Weekend, a popular annual event for goths and other alternative subcultures.

Whitby was founded in the 7th century by St. Hilda, and the town grew in importance as a fishing port and a center for the wool trade. The abbey was founded in the 11th century and was one of the most important religious centers in England. The abbey was dissolved in the 16th century, but the ruins remain a popular tourist attraction.

The town's narrow streets are lined with shops, cafes, and pubs. The most famous street in Whitby is Church Street, which leads up to the abbey. Church Street is a steep climb, but the views from the top are worth it.

Whitby is also a popular destination for hikers and bikers. There are several trails that lead up to the abbey, and there are also trails that follow the coastline.

If you're looking for a unique and atmospheric place to visit in Yorkshire, then Whitby is definitely worth a visit.

Here are some of the things you can do in Whitby:

Visit the abbey ruins: The abbey ruins are one of the most popular tourist attractions in Whitby. You can climb to the top of the ruins for stunning views of the town and the North Sea.

Explore the town's narrow streets: Whitby's narrow streets are lined with shops, cafes, and pubs. See what you can find by taking a stroll through the streets.

Go hiking or biking: There are several trails that lead up to the abbey, and there are also trails that follow the coastline. If you're looking for a more active way to explore Whitby, then hiking or biking is a great option.

Take a boat trip: There are several boat trips that depart from Whitby harbour. You can take a boat trip to see the seals, or you can take a boat trip to Robin Hood's Bay.

Visit the Whitby Museum: The Whitby Museum is a great place to learn about the history of Whitby. The museum has exhibits on the abbey, the fishing industry, and the town's role in the Industrial Revolution.

Attend the Whitby Goth Weekend: The Whitby Goth Weekend is a popular annual event for goths and other alternative subcultures. The event takes place over the weekend of Halloween, and it features live music, fashion shows, and other events.

Here are some tips for visiting Whitby:

Visit in the spring or fall: The weather is mild in the spring and fall, making it a great time to visit Whitby.

Wear comfortable shoes: You'll be doing a lot of walking in Whitby, so make sure you wear comfortable shoes.

Bring a camera: There are many photo opportunities in Whitby, so make sure you bring a camera.

Be prepared for rain: The weather in Whitby can be unpredictable, so be prepared for rain.

5.3.2. Scarborough

North Yorkshire, England's Scarborough, is a seaside community. About 25 miles (40 km) east of York, it is situated on the North Sea shore. The town has a lengthy past that dates to the Roman era. It was a well-liked resort for the affluent in the 18th and 19th centuries, and it is still a well-liked tourist destination today.

Scarborough is a vibrant town with a lot to offer visitors. There are beautiful beaches, historic landmarks, and plenty of things to do. Some of the most popular attractions in Scarborough include:

Scarborough Castle (): One of Scarborough's most recognizable landmarks is this castle from the 12th century. It provides breathtaking views of the town and the countryside beyond. William the Conqueror erected the castle in 1139 to defend the town from invasion. Over the ages, it has seen numerous expansions and reconstructions, and now it is a well-liked tourist destination.

The Spa: Scarborough is home to one of the oldest spas in England. The spa has been in operation since the 17th century, and it offers a variety of treatments, including bathing, massage, and beauty treatments. The spa is located in the heart of the town, and it is surrounded by beautiful gardens.

Scarborough Open Air Theatre: This open-air theatre is one of the largest in the UK. It hosts a variety of performances, including plays, musicals, and concerts. The theatre is located on the South Cliff, and it has a capacity of over 8,000 people.

Scarborough Museum: This museum tells the story of Scarborough from its earliest days to the present. It houses a collection of artifacts, documents, and photographs that illustrate the town's rich history. The museum is located in the town center, and it is open to the public all year round.

North Bay: This is the most popular beach in Scarborough. It is a long, sandy beach with plenty of space for swimming, sunbathing, and playing. The beach is located on the North side of the town, and it is easily accessible by foot or by bus.

South Bay: This is a smaller beach than North Bay, but it is just as charming. It is a good place to go for a quiet swim or a walk along the seafront. The beach is located on the South side of the town, and it is easily accessible by foot or by bus.

In addition to these attractions, Scarborough also has a vibrant nightlife scene. There are plenty of bars, clubs, and restaurants to choose from, so you are sure to find something to your taste.

If you are looking for a fun and exciting seaside town to visit, Scarborough is a great option. It has something to offer everyone, from history buffs to beach lovers to partygoers.

Here are some additional tips for planning your trip to Scarborough:

The best time to visit Scarborough is during the summer months, when the weather is warm and sunny. However, the town is also a popular destination during the spring and autumn, when the crowds are smaller.

If you are planning on visiting Scarborough during the summer, be sure to book your accommodation well in advance. The town can get very busy during this time, and it can be difficult to find a place to stay.

There are a variety of ways to get to Scarborough. You can drive, take the train, or fly. The nearest airport is Leeds Bradford Airport, which is about an hour's drive from Scarborough.

Once you are in Scarborough, you can get around by foot, bicycle, or bus. The town is compact and easy to walk around, but there are also plenty of bus routes that can take you to all the major attractions.

5.3.3. Filey

Filey is a seaside town on the North Yorkshire coast, about 20 miles from York. It is a popular holiday destination, thanks to its long sandy beaches, mild climate, and abundance of family-friendly attractions.

The main beach in Filey is South Beach, which is about two miles long. It is a Blue Flag beach, which means it meets strict environmental standards. The beach is backed by dunes, which provide a haven for wildlife.

There are plenty of activities to enjoy on South Beach, including swimming, sunbathing, sandcastle building, and surfing. There are also a number of beachside cafes and restaurants, where you can enjoy a bite to eat or a drink.

If you are looking for something a little different, you can visit Filey Brigg, which is a headland that juts out into the North Sea. The Brigg offers stunning views of the coastline, and there are a number of walking trails that you can follow.

Filey also has a number of other attractions, including Filey Museum, which tells the story of the town's history; Filey Winter Gardens, which are a beautiful set of Victorian glasshouses; and Filey Mere, which is a freshwater lake that is popular for fishing and boating.

If you are looking for a place to stay in Filey, there are a number of hotels, guesthouses, and caravan parks to choose from. There are also a number of self-catering apartments and cottages available.

Filey is a great place to visit any time of year, but it is particularly popular during the summer months. If you are looking for a relaxing beach holiday with plenty of family-friendly activities, then Filey is a great option.

Here are some additional tips for your visit to Filey:

The best time to visit Filey is during the summer months, when the weather is warm and sunny. However, the town is also a popular destination during the spring and autumn.

If you are planning on visiting Filey during the peak season, it is advisable to book your accommodation in advance.

There are a number of car parks in Filey, but they can get busy during the summer months. If you are planning on driving to Filey, it is advisable to arrive early or late in the day to avoid the crowds.

There are a number of bus services that operate to Filey from York, Scarborough, and other towns in the area.

Filey is a very walkable town, so you can easily explore the town centre and the beach on foot.

There are a number of places to eat in Filey, ranging from cafes and restaurants to fish and chip shops.

Filey is a great place to visit for families, as there are a number of family-friendly attractions, including the beach, the Brigg, and the Winter Gardens.

5.4. Rural Retreats

5.4.1. Haworth

Haworth is a village in the Yorkshire Dales, England. It is famous for its association with the Brontë sisters, who lived there in the 19th century. The village is home to the Brontë Parsonage Museum, which is a must-visit for fans of the Brontës. Other attractions in Haworth include the Haworth Moors, the Keighley and Worth Valley Railway, and the Brontë Waterfall.

Haworth is a lovely community with a lengthy past. It was originally a prosperous wool town, and the 17th and 18th century homes line the steep, cobblestone alleys. The Bront sisters were christened in St. Michael's Church, one of the many churches in the village.

The Brontë Parsonage Museum is the most popular tourist attraction in Haworth. It was the home of the Brontë family from 1820 to 1861, and it is now a museum dedicated to their lives and work. The museum houses a collection of the Brontë sisters' manuscripts, letters, and personal belongings. It also has a number of exhibits on the history of Haworth and the Brontë family.

The Haworth Moors are a popular spot for hiking, biking, and walking. The moors offer stunning views of the surrounding countryside, and they are home to a variety of wildlife, including grouse, rabbits, and foxes.

The Keighley and Worth Valley Railway is a narrow-gauge railway that runs through the Yorkshire Dales. The railway offers a scenic journey between Haworth and Keighley, and it is a popular tourist attraction.

The Brontë Waterfall is a small waterfall located near Haworth. The waterfall is a popular spot for picnics and swimming, and it is a beautiful place to visit in the summertime.

Haworth is a charming village with a lot to offer visitors. Whether you are a fan of the Brontë sisters or you are simply looking for a beautiful place to visit, Haworth is a great place to spend a day or two.

Here are some other things to do in Haworth:

Visit the Brontë Waterfall
Take a walk on the Haworth Moors
Visit the Keighley and Worth Valley Railway
Go shopping in Haworth's independent shops
Enjoy a traditional Yorkshire tea at one of Haworth's cafes
Visit the Brontë Parsonage Museum
Attend the Haworth Festival, which is held every year in July

Haworth is a great place to visit any time of year, but it is especially beautiful in the spring and fall. The village is also a popular destination for Christmas, as it is decorated with festive lights and decorations.

If you are planning a visit to Haworth, I recommend staying at one of the village's many bed and breakfasts. This will give you a chance to experience the unique charm of Haworth and to walk in the footsteps of the Brontë sisters.

5.4.2. Ripon

Ripon is a beautiful city in North Yorkshire, England. It is known for its cathedral, which is one of the oldest in the country. Ripon is also a popular destination for walkers and cyclists. There are many beautiful walks and cycle routes in the surrounding countryside. If you are looking for a relaxing and scenic getaway, Ripon is the perfect place for you.

History

Ripon was founded in the 7th century by King Edwin of Northumbria. The city was originally called Hrypetun, which means "settlement on the River Hreope". Ripon was an important religious center in the Middle Ages, and the cathedral was built in the 12th century. The city was also a major market town, and it was granted a royal charter in 1189.

Cathedral

Ripon Cathedral is one of the oldest cathedrals in England. It was built in the 12th century, and it is a beautiful example of Norman architecture. The cathedral has a long and rich history, and it has been the site of many important events over the centuries.

Walks and Cycle Routes

There are many beautiful walks and cycle routes in the surrounding countryside. Some of the most popular walks include the Ripon Rowel, the Nidd Gorge Walk, and the Fountains Abbey Walk. There are also many cycle routes, including the Great North Rail Trail and the Nidderdale Way.

Things to Do

In addition to visiting the cathedral, there are many other things to do in Ripon. Some of the most popular attractions include the Ripon Museum, the Ripon Racecourse, and the Ripon Farmers' Market. There are also many pubs and restaurants in Ripon, where you can enjoy traditional Yorkshire food and drink.

Getting There

Ripon is well-connected by road and rail. The nearest major airport is Leeds Bradford Airport, which is about an hour's drive away. There are also regular train services from Leeds and York.

Accommodation

There are many different types of accommodation available in Ripon, including hotels, bed and breakfasts, and self-catering apartments. There are also a number of campsites in the surrounding countryside.

Ripon is a beautiful and historic city with a lot to offer visitors. Whether you are interested in history, culture, or the outdoors, you are sure to find something to enjoy in Ripon.

Here are some additional details about Ripon:

The population of Ripon is about 15,000 people.
The city is located on the River Ure, which is a tributary of the River Ouse.
In North Yorkshire, Ripon serves as the county seat.
The city is home to a number of businesses, including a brewery, a chocolate factory, and a furniture manufacturer.
Ripon is also a popular tourist destination, and it is known for its cathedral, its walks and cycle routes, and its traditional Yorkshire food and drink.

5.4.3. Harrogate

Harrogate is a beautiful spa town in North Yorkshire, England. It is known for its thermal springs, which have been used for centuries for their healing properties. The town is also home to a number of parks and gardens, as well as a variety of cultural attractions, including theaters, museums, and art galleries.

Harrogate is a great place to relax and escape the hustle and bustle of everyday life. There are plenty of things to do in the town, but it is also easy to find peace and quiet in one of the many parks or gardens. If you are looking for a relaxing spa break, Harrogate is the perfect destination.

Things to do in Harrogate

Visit the Pump Room: The Pump Room is where the town's thermal springs are located. You can take a tour of the room, or sample the spa water.

Explore the parks and gardens: Harrogate is home to a number of beautiful parks and gardens, including Valley Gardens, Harlow Carr, and The Stray.

Visit the museums and art galleries: Harrogate has a number of museums and art galleries, including the Yorkshire Dales National Park Museum, the Royal Pump Room Museum, and the Mercer Art Gallery.

Go shopping: Harrogate is a great place to go shopping. There are a number of independent shops in the town, as well as a number of chain stores.

See a show: Harrogate has a number of theaters, including the Royal Hall and the Theatre Royal. There are always a variety of shows on, from plays to musicals to concerts.

Take a walk or hike: Harrogate is surrounded by beautiful countryside. There are a number of walking and hiking trails in the area, including the Nidd Gorge Walk and the South of the Dales Walk.

Where to stay in Harrogate

There are a number of hotels, guesthouses, and bed and breakfasts in Harrogate. Some of the most popular hotels include the Royal Hotel, the Crown Hotel, and the Old Swan Hotel.

Getting to Harrogate

Harrogate is easily accessible by train, bus, and car. The train station is located in the town center, and there are regular trains from Leeds, York, and Manchester. The bus station is also located in the town center, and there are regular buses from surrounding towns and villages. If you are driving, there are a number of car parks in the town center.

Harrogate is a great place to visit any time of year. The town is particularly beautiful in the spring and summer, when the parks and gardens are in full bloom. However, Harrogate is also a popular destination in the winter, when the town is transformed into a winter wonderland.

6. Planning Your Trip To Yorkshire

6.1. Best Time to Visit

There are certain seasons of the year that are preferable to others for particular activities.

Spring (March-May)

Spring is a great time to visit Yorkshire if you're looking for milder weather and fewer crowds. The days are getting longer, and the flowers are starting to bloom, making for some stunning scenery. This is also a good time to go hiking or biking in the Yorkshire Dales or the North York Moors National Parks.

Summer (June-August)

Summer is the peak season for tourism in Yorkshire, and for good reason. The weather is warm and sunny, and there are plenty of outdoor activities to enjoy. This is a great time to visit the beaches, go sailing, or hike in the hills. However, it's also the busiest time of year, so be prepared for crowds.

Autumn (September-November)

Autumn is a beautiful time of year in Yorkshire. The leaves start to change color, and the weather is still mild. This is a great time to go on a scenic drive through the countryside or visit one of the many stately homes or gardens.

Winter (December-February)

Winter in Yorkshire can be cold and snowy, but it's also a magical time of year. The Christmas markets are in full swing, and there are plenty of opportunities to go sledding, ice skating, or skiing. If you're looking for a winter wonderland, Yorkshire is the place to be.

Ultimately, the best time to visit Yorkshire depends on your personal preferences. If you're looking for warm weather and plenty of activities, summer is a great time to go. If you prefer milder weather and fewer crowds, spring or autumn are better options. And if you want to experience a winter wonderland, winter is the time for you.

6.2. Duration of Stay

The duration of your stay in Yorkshire will depend on your interests and how much you want to see and do. If you are only interested in visiting the major cities, such as York and Leeds, then you could get away with a short trip of 2-3 days. However, if you want to explore the countryside and national parks, then you will need a longer trip of 5-7 days or more.

Here is a suggested itinerary for a 7-day trip to Yorkshire:

Day 1: Arrive in York and check into your hotel.

Day 2: Explore the city of York, including York Minster, the Shambles, and the National Railway Museum.

Day 3: Take a day trip to the Yorkshire Dales, hiking in the countryside or visiting some of the small villages.

Day 4: Visit Fountains Abbey and Studley Royal Water Gardens, a UNESCO World Heritage Site.

Day 5: Drive to the North York Moors National Park, stopping at Robin Hood's Bay and Whitby along the way.

Day 6: Hike on the North York Moors, visit Rievaulx Abbey, or take a ride on the North Yorkshire Moors Railway.

Day 7: Depart from York.

This is just a suggested itinerary, of course, and you can tailor it to your own interests. If you are interested in history, you could spend more time visiting castles and stately homes. If you are interested in nature, you could spend more time hiking and exploring the national parks.

No matter how long you stay in Yorkshire, you are sure to have a memorable trip. The county has something to offer everyone, from history lovers to nature lovers to foodies.

6.3. Accommodation Options

There are a wide variety of accommodation options available in Yorkshire, to suit all budgets and tastes. Here are a few of the most popular options:

Hotels: There are hotels of all sizes and price points in Yorkshire, from budget-friendly chains to luxurious boutique hotels. Some of the most popular hotels in Yorkshire include The Principal York, The Grand Hotel York, and The Deansgate Hotel Harrogate.

Bed and breakfasts: Bed and breakfasts (B&Bs) are a great way to experience the local culture and hospitality. B&Bs can be found in all parts of Yorkshire, from small villages to bustling towns. Some of the best B&Bs in

Yorkshire include The Old Vicarage Malham, The Old Forge Inn & Rooms Settle, and The White Lion Hotel & Spa Skipton.

Apartments: Apartments are a great option for families or groups of friends. Apartments can be rented by the night, week, or month. Some of the best apartment rental companies in Yorkshire include Sykes Holiday Cottages, Staycity, and The Apartment Network.

Camping: Camping is a great way to experience the great outdoors in Yorkshire. There are campsites to suit all budgets and styles, from basic campsites to luxury glamping sites. Some of the best campsites in Yorkshire include Nidderdale Camping & Caravanning Park, Malham Tarn Campsite, and Brimham Rocks Camping.

Hostels: Hostels are a great option for budget travelers. Hostels offer shared dormitories and private rooms, as well as communal kitchen and laundry facilities. Some of the best hostels in Yorkshire include YHA York, YHA Malham, and YHA Ilkley.

When choosing accommodation in Yorkshire, it is important to consider your budget, your travel style, and the specific activities you plan to do. For example, if you are planning on doing a lot of hiking and camping, you will need to choose accommodation that is close to the trails. If you are traveling with children, you may want to choose an accommodation that has family-friendly amenities, such as a playground or pool.

No matter what your budget or travel style, you are sure to find the perfect accommodation in Yorkshire. With so many options to choose from, you are sure to find a place that you will love.

Here are some additional tips for choosing accommodation in Yorkshire:

Book early: Accommodation in Yorkshire can be popular, especially during peak season. To avoid disappointment, it is a good idea to book your accommodation early.

Consider the location: Where you stay in Yorkshire will have a big impact on your trip. If you are interested in hiking and outdoor activities, you will want to choose accommodation that is close to the trails. If you are interested in visiting historical sites, you will want to choose accommodation that is close to the cities.

Read reviews: Before you book your accommodation, be sure to read the reviews. You can get a decent indication of what other visitors have encountered by doing this.

Be flexible: If you are flexible with your dates and your budget, you are more likely to find a great deal on accommodation.

6.4. Transportation within Yorkshire

There are a variety of ways to get around Yorkshire, depending on your budget and preferences. Some of the more well-liked choices are as follows:

Train: The National Rail network provides excellent coverage of Yorkshire, with trains connecting all of the major cities and towns. You can buy tickets online, at train stations, or from ticket machines.

Bus: Buses are a more affordable option than trains, and they can be a good way to get to smaller towns and villages. The main bus operator in Yorkshire is First Bus, but there are also a number of smaller companies that operate services in specific areas.

Car: If you're planning on doing a lot of driving, it can be a good idea to hire a car. This gives you the freedom to explore at your own pace and to visit places that are not well-served by public transport.

Taxi: Taxis can be a convenient way to get around, but they can be expensive. They're a good option if you're short on time or if you're traveling with a group of people.

Shared transport: There are a number of shared transport schemes operating in Yorkshire, such as Liftshare and BlaBlaCar. These schemes allow you to connect with other people who are traveling to the same destination as you, and they can be a great way to save money on your travel costs.

If you're planning on doing a lot of hiking or exploring the countryside, you may also want to consider renting a bike. There are a number of bike rental companies operating in Yorkshire, and this can be a great way to get around and see the sights at your own pace.

Here are some additional tips for planning your transportation within Yorkshire:

Book your tickets in advance: This is especially important if you're traveling during peak season or if you're planning on taking a train.

Consider your budget: If you're on a tight budget, you may want to consider taking the bus or cycling.

Plan your route: This will help you to make the most of your time and to avoid unnecessary backtracking.

Be flexible: Things don't always go according to plan, so it's a good idea to be flexible with your transportation arrangements.

7. Top Attractions and Landmarks in Yorkshire

7.1. York Minster

York Minster is one of the most popular tourist attractions in Yorkshire, and for good reason. It is the largest Gothic cathedral in Northern Europe, and its stunning architecture is sure to take your breath away.

The history of York Minster dates back to the 7th century, when a small church was built on the site. The current cathedral was begun in the 12th century, and it took over 200 years to complete. The cathedral has been restored and modified many times over the centuries, but it still retains its original Gothic style.

One of the most striking features of York Minster is its West Front, which is decorated with intricate carvings. The West Front is divided into three levels, each of which is filled with statues and other religious imagery. The uppermost level features a large rose window, which is one of the largest in England.

The interior of York Minster is just as impressive as the exterior. The nave is incredibly tall and spacious, and the ceiling is decorated with beautiful stained glass windows. The cathedral also contains a number of other treasures, including a 13th-century astronomical clock, a 14th-century misericord, and a 15th-century choir screen.

York Minster is a UNESCO World Heritage Site, and it is one of the most popular tourist destinations in the UK. The cathedral is open to visitors all year round, and there are a number of guided tours available.

Things to do at York Minster:

Explore the cathedral's interior, including the nave, the choir, and the West Front.

Admire the stained glass windows.

Visit the Chapter House, where the York Chapter met.

See the astronomical clock.

Learn about the cathedral's history on a guided tour.

Attend a service or concert.

Take a walk around the cathedral's grounds.

Tips for visiting York Minster:

Buy your tickets in advance, especially if you are visiting during peak season.

Dress appropriately. The cathedral is a place of worship, so you should dress modestly.

Be respectful of the other visitors. The cathedral is a place of peace and quiet, so please be mindful of your noise levels.

* Take your time exploring the cathedral. Since there is a lot to see and do, you shouldn't rush.

How to go to York Minster:

The York Minster is situated in the center of York. It is accessible by automobile, bus, or train. Just outside the cathedral, there is a parking lot, and several bus stops are close by. The cathedral is a short distance from York station, which is the closest train station.

Other sights and activities in York include:

The Shambles: A historic street with timber-framed buildings.
Clifford's Tower: A medieval castle.
The Jorvik Viking Centre: A museum that tells the story of York's Viking past.
The National Railway Museum: A museum that houses a collection of historic locomotives and railway carriages.
The Yorkshire Museum: A museum that tells the story of Yorkshire's history and culture.

7.2. The Yorkshire Sculpture Park

The Yorkshire Sculpture Park (YSP) is one of the most popular tourist attractions in Yorkshire, England. It is home to an extensive collection of modern and contemporary sculptures, which are displayed in a stunning natural setting. The park is also a popular destination for events, such as concerts, festivals, and workshops.

The YSP was founded in 1977 by Peter Murray, who was inspired by the idea of creating a sculpture park in the English countryside. The park's first exhibition was held in 1978, and it has since grown to become one of the most important sculpture parks in the world.

The YSP's collection includes over 3,000 works of art, by artists from around the world. Some of the most well-known sculptures in the collection include Henry Moore's "Two Piece Reclining Figure No. 1" (1969), Anthony Caro's "Early One Morning" (1962), and Barbara

Hepworth's "Two Forms (Divided Circle)" (1969).

The sculptures are displayed in a variety of settings, including woodland, meadows, and lakes. This allows visitors to experience the art in a natural way, and to interact with it in a more personal way.

In addition to its collection of sculptures, the YSP also offers a variety of other attractions, including a learning center, a café, and a shop. The learning center offers a variety of educational programs for all ages, from school children to adults. The café is a great place to relax and enjoy a bite to eat, and the shop sells a variety of souvenirs and gifts.

The YSP is open all year round, and admission is charged. However, there are a number of free events held throughout the year, such as concerts, festivals, and workshops.

The Yorkshire Sculpture Park is a truly unique and special place. It is a place where art and nature come together in perfect harmony. It is a place where visitors can relax and enjoy the beauty of the outdoors, while also being inspired by the work of some of the world's greatest artists.

Here are some additional details about the Yorkshire Sculpture Park:

 The park is located in West Bretton, Wakefield, West Yorkshire.
 It is open from 10am to 5pm daily, from March to October, and from 11am to 4pm daily, from November to February.
 Admission is £12.50 for adults, £9.50 for concessions, and free for children under 16.
 A café and a store are located there. Train, bus, and automobiles can all take you to the park.

Visitor advice for the Yorkshire Sculpture Park is provided below:

 Take your time exploring the park. You won't want to rush through because there are almost

3,000 pieces of art on show. Put on some relaxed shoes. The process of touring the park involves a lot of walking.

Bring lunch for a picnic. In the park, there are several places to relax and eat.

Visit during the spring or fall. The park is less crowded during these times of year.

Take a guided tour. This is a great way to learn more about the park's history and collection.

7.3. Fountains Abbey and Studley Royal Water Garden

Fountains Abbey and Studley Royal Water Garden is a UNESCO World Heritage Site in North Yorkshire, England. It is a beautiful and tranquil place, consisting of a ruined abbey, a large water garden, and extensive parkland.

The abbey was founded in 1132 by Cistercian monks, and it quickly became one of the most important religious houses in England. The abbey was dissolved in 1539 during the Dissolution of the Monasteries, but the ruins remain a popular tourist destination.

The water garden was created in the 17th and 18th centuries, and it is one of the finest examples of its kind in the world. The garden is designed to reflect the changing seasons, and it is full of beautiful flowers, trees, and fountains.

The parkland surrounding the abbey and water garden is also worth exploring. There are miles of walking trails, and you can often see deer, foxes, and other wildlife.

Fountains Abbey and Studley Royal Water Garden is a truly special place, and it is a must-visit for anyone interested in history, nature, or beauty.

History

Fountains Abbey was founded in 1132 by Cistercian monks from Rievaulx Abbey. The monks chose the site for its beauty and isolation, and they soon began to build a thriving community.

The abbey was built in the Gothic style, and it was one of the largest and most impressive abbeys in England. The abbey church was over 500 feet long, and it had a nave that was 100 feet high. The abbey also had a number of other buildings, including a cloister, a chapter house, and a dormitory.

The abbey prospered for centuries, but it was dissolved in 1539 during the Dissolution of the Monasteries. The abbey's lands were sold to private individuals, and the buildings were left to ruin.

Water Garden

The water garden at Fountains Abbey was created in the 17th and 18th centuries. The garden was designed by John Aislabie, a wealthy landowner who was also the Chancellor of the Exchequer. Aislabie was inspired by the Italian Renaissance gardens, and he created a garden that was full of beautiful flowers, trees, and fountains.

The water garden is divided into two parts: the Upper Garden and the Lower Garden. The Upper Garden is located on the site of the former abbey orchard, and it is full of formal gardens, fountains, and statues. The Lower Garden is located in the valley below the abbey, and it is a more natural garden with winding paths, lakes, and waterfalls.

Parkland

The parkland surrounding Fountains Abbey and Studley Royal Water Garden is also worth exploring. There are miles of walking trails, and you can often see deer, foxes, and other wildlife.

The parkland was created in the 18th century, and it is designed to reflect the changing seasons. In the spring, the parkland is full of wildflowers, and in the summer, the trees are full of leaves. In the autumn, the leaves turn a beautiful shade of orange, and in the winter, the parkland is covered in snow.

Things to Do

There are a number of things to do at Fountains Abbey and Studley Royal Water Garden. You can visit the ruins of the abbey, explore the water garden, or walk in the parkland. There are also a number of guided tours available, and you can even rent a boat to explore the lakes.

Getting There

Fountains Abbey and Studley Royal Water Garden is located in the village of Fountains Abbey, North Yorkshire. The nearest town is Ripon, which is about 3 miles away.

The abbey is open to the public all year round, and admission is charged. There are also a number of parking spaces available at the abbey.

Tips

If you are visiting in the summer, it is advisable to arrive early, as the abbey can get very busy.

There are a number of different trails in the parkland, so you can choose one that suits your fitness level.

If you are interested in learning more about the abbey's history, there are a number of guided tours available.

Fountains Abbey and Studley Royal Water Garden is a truly special place, and it is a must-visit for anyone interested in history, nature, or beauty. The abbey ruins are stunning, the water garden is a delight, and the parkland is a peaceful oasis. Whether you are a history buff, a nature lover, or simply someone who appreciates beauty, you will find something to love.

7.4. Bolton Abbey

Bolton Abbey is a 12th-century abbey in the Yorkshire Dales National Park, England. It is one of the most popular tourist attractions in the park, and is known for its beautiful setting, its historic buildings, and its stunning scenery.

The abbey was founded in 1152 by Henry Murdac, the Archbishop of York. It was originally a Benedictine monastery, but it was dissolved by Henry VIII in 1539. The abbey buildings were then sold to private owners, and they have been in various states of repair ever since.

The abbey today is a mixture of ruins and restored buildings. The most impressive part of the abbey is the 13th-century church, which is still largely intact. The church has a beautiful nave and choir, and it is topped by a soaring tower.

The abbey is also surrounded by beautiful countryside. The River Wharfe flows past the abbey, and there are several waterfalls in the area. There are also several trails that lead through the surrounding countryside, offering stunning views of the abbey and the surrounding hills.

In addition to its historic buildings and stunning scenery, Bolton Abbey is also home to a variety of wildlife. The park is home to deer, foxes, badgers, and many other animals. There are also several bird species that can be seen in the area, including kingfishers, swallows, and owls.

Bolton Abbey is a popular destination for both daytrippers and overnight visitors. There is a car park near the abbey, and there are also several hotels and restaurants in the area.

Things to do at Bolton Abbey

Visit the abbey ruins: The abbey ruins are the main attraction at Bolton Abbey. You can walk around the ruins and explore the different parts of the church.

Go for a walk: There are several trails that lead through the surrounding countryside. These trails offer stunning views of the abbey and the surrounding hills.

Go fishing: The River Wharfe is a popular spot for fishing. Salmon, trout, and more species are available for fishing.

Visit the Strid: The Strid is a narrow gorge that is located near the abbey. It is a popular spot for photographers and for people who enjoy exploring the natural landscape.

Have a picnic: There are several picnic areas near the abbey. This is a great place to enjoy a meal in the fresh air.

How to get to Bolton Abbey

Bolton Abbey is located in the Yorkshire Dales National Park, about 10 miles south of Skipton. The nearest train station is at Skipton, and there is a bus service that runs from Skipton to Bolton Abbey.

If you are driving, there is a car park near the abbey. The postcode for the car park is BD23 6EX.

Opening hours and admission prices

The abbey is open all year round, but the opening hours vary depending on the time of year. The abbey is usually open from 9:30am to 5pm, but it is open later in the summer months.

Admission prices to the abbey are:

Adults: £8.50
Children (5-16): £4.50
Family ticket (2 adults + 3 children): £23

There are also reduced admission prices for seniors and students.

Tips for visiting Bolton Abbey

Visit during the spring or autumn for the best weather.

Wear comfortable shoes as there is a lot of walking involved.

Bring a picnic lunch to enjoy in the abbey grounds.

If you are visiting in the summer, be sure to book your tickets in advance.

Overall, Bolton Abbey is a beautiful and historic place that is well worth a visit. It is a great place to relax and enjoy the stunning scenery, and there are plenty of things to do for people of all ages.

7.5. Whitby Abbey

Whitby Abbey is one of the most iconic landmarks in Yorkshire, and for good reason. The ruins of this once-great abbey sit perched on a cliff overlooking the North Sea, making for a truly stunning sight.

The abbey was founded in 657 AD by St. Hilda, and it quickly became one of the most important religious centers in England. It was also a major center of learning, and it is said that Bede the Venerable studied here.

The abbey was destroyed by fire in 1540, during the Dissolution of the Monasteries. However, the ruins have been carefully preserved, and they are now a popular tourist destination.

There are a number of things to see and do at Whitby Abbey. You can explore the ruins, visit the abbey museum, or take a walk along the clifftop. The abbey is also a popular spot for photography, and the views from the top are simply breathtaking.

If you're looking for a truly unique and memorable experience, then a visit to Whitby Abbey is a must.

History of Whitby Abbey

Whitby Abbey was founded in 657 AD by St. Hilda, the daughter of King Edwin of

Northumbria. The abbey was originally built as a monastery for Benedictine monks, but it was later converted into a nunnery.

Whitby Abbey was a major center of learning during the Middle Ages. It was here that Bede the Venerable, one of the most important scholars of the early Middle Ages, studied. Bede wrote his famous Ecclesiastical History of the English People at Whitby Abbey.

The abbey was destroyed by fire in 1540, during the Dissolution of the Monasteries. However, the ruins have been carefully preserved, and they are now a popular tourist destination.

Things to do at Whitby Abbey

There are a number of things to see and do at Whitby Abbey. You can explore the ruins, visit the abbey museum, or take a walk along the clifftop. The abbey is also a popular spot for photography, and the views from the top are simply breathtaking.

Explore the ruins: The ruins of Whitby Abbey are a fascinating place to explore. You can wander through the old cloisters, see the ruins of the church, and even climb to the top of the bell tower for panoramic views of the surrounding area.

Visit the abbey museum: The abbey museum tells the story of Whitby Abbey from its founding to its destruction. You can see exhibits on the abbey's history, its architecture, and its role in English culture.

Take a walk along the clifftop: The clifftop walk at Whitby Abbey is one of the most popular things to do in the area. The views from the top are simply stunning, and you can often see seals and other wildlife in the water below.

How to get to Whitby Abbey

Whitby Abbey is located in the town of Whitby, in North Yorkshire, England. The abbey is about a 2-hour drive from York, and it's also accessible by train.

If you're driving, you'll need to follow the A19 to Whitby. Once you reach Whitby, follow the signs to the abbey.

If you're taking the train, you'll need to get off at Whitby station. From the station, it's a short walk to the abbey.

Opening hours and admission prices

Whitby Abbey is open from 10am to 5pm, seven days a week. Admission prices are:

Adults: £10
Seniors (65+): £8
Children (5-16): £5
Family (2 adults + 2 children): £25

Tips for visiting Whitby Abbey

Be sure to wear comfortable shoes, as there is a lot of walking involved.
If you're visiting in the summer, be prepared for crowds.

Bring a camera, as you'll want to capture the beauty of the ruins.

If you're interested in learning more about the abbey's history, be sure to visit the abbey museum.

7.6. Harewood House

Harewood House is a Grade I listed country house in Harewood, West Yorkshire, England. It is the home of the Lascelles family, and has been since 1699. The house is set in 2,000 acres of parkland, and is one of the most popular tourist attractions in Yorkshire.

The house was built in the early 18th century by the 1st Earl of Harewood, Henry Lascelles. He commissioned the architect John Carr to design a Palladian-style mansion, and the house was completed in 1712. The interior of the house is lavishly decorated, with a number of fine paintings, sculptures, and furniture.

One of the most notable features of Harewood House is its collection of Chippendale furniture. The 1st Earl of Harewood was a great admirer of Thomas Chippendale, and he commissioned the furniture maker to create a number of pieces for the house. The collection includes some of Chippendale's most famous pieces, such as the Harewood Dressing Table and the Harewood Bookcase.

Another highlight of Harewood House is its library. The library was built in the 1780s, and it contains over 10,000 books. The library is decorated with a number of fine paintings, and it is one of the most beautiful libraries in England.

The gardens at Harewood House are also worth seeing. The gardens were designed by Capability Brown, and they are considered to be one of the finest examples of his work. The gardens include a number of different features, such as a lake, a waterfall, and a number of follies.

Harewood House is open to the public, and it is a popular destination for tourists and locals alike. The house offers a number of different tours, including guided tours, self-guided tours, and family-friendly tours. The house also hosts a number of events throughout the year, such as concerts, exhibitions, and festivals.

Things to do at Harewood House

- Explore the house and gardens
- Take a guided tour
- Visit the library
- Enjoy a picnic in the gardens
- Attend an event
- Go shopping in the gift shop

How to get to Harewood House

Harewood House is located in Harewood, West Yorkshire, England. The nearest train station is Harewood Station, which is about a 10-minute walk from the house. The house is also accessible by car, and there is a car park on site.

Opening hours and admission prices

Harewood House is open from 10am to 5pm, seven days a week. Admission prices are £18 for adults, £12 for children, and £16 for concessions. There are also family tickets available.

Tips for visiting Harewood House

Book your tickets in advance, especially if you are visiting during peak season.
Allow plenty of time to explore the house and gardens.
Since there will be a lot of walking, wear cozy shoes.
Bring a picnic lunch to enjoy in the gardens.
Visit the gift shop for souvenirs.

Harewood House is a beautiful and historic house that is well worth a visit. The house is full of interesting things to see and do, and the gardens are stunning. Whether you are interested in history, art, or simply enjoying the outdoors, you are sure to find something to enjoy at Harewood House.

7.7. Castle Howard

Castle Howard is one of the most popular tourist attractions in Yorkshire, and for good reason. This magnificent stately home is a stunning example of Georgian architecture, and its sprawling grounds are home to a variety of gardens, lakes, and follies.

Castle Howard was built in the early 18th century by Charles Howard, the 3rd Earl of Carlisle. The earl was a great admirer of Italian Baroque architecture, and he commissioned the architect Nicholas Hawksmoor to design a house that would rival the great palaces of Italy.

The result was a truly spectacular building. Castle Howard is a vast structure, with over 1,000 rooms. The exterior is made of limestone, and it is decorated with a profusion of columns, balustrades, and pediments. The interior is just as impressive, with lavishly decorated rooms, a grand staircase, and a beautiful chapel.

In addition to the house itself, the grounds of Castle Howard are also worth exploring. The gardens are a series of formal terraces, lawns, and lakes. There are also a number of follies scattered throughout the grounds, including a ruined abbey, a Gothic temple, and a Chinese pagoda.

Castle Howard is a truly magical place, and it is no wonder that it has been used as a filming location for a number of movies and television shows. It has appeared in films such as "Brideshead Revisited" and "The Remains of the Day," and it has also been used in the television series "Downton Abbey."

If you are visiting Yorkshire, be sure to add Castle Howard to your list of must-see attractions. It is a truly unforgettable place.

Here are some additional details about Castle Howard:

The home was constructed between 1699 and 1712.
It is situated in a parks area with 1,000 acres.
The gardens were designed by Charles Bridgeman and William Kent.
The house has been home to the Howard family for over 300 years.
It is a popular filming location for movies and television shows.

Here are some tips for visiting Castle Howard:

Allow at least 3 hours to explore the house and gardens.
It involves a lot of walking, so wear comfortable shoes. Bring a camera to record the breathtaking sights. Visit the gardens in the spring or fall while they are blooming.

Purchase your tickets in advance, particularly if you are traveling during a popular time of year.

Castle Howard is a truly magical place, and it is a must-see for any visitor to Yorkshire. With its stunning architecture, beautiful gardens, and fascinating history, it is sure to leave a lasting impression.

8. Outdoor Activities and Adventure in Yorkshire

8.1. Hiking and Walking Trails

Yorkshire is a hiker's paradise. With its rolling hills, towering peaks, and dramatic coastline, there are endless trails to explore. Whether you're looking for a leisurely stroll or a challenging hike, you're sure to find something to your liking.

Here are a few of the most popular hiking and walking trails in Yorkshire:

Malham Tarn Circular Walk: This 10-kilometer loop takes you around the stunning Malham Tarn, a glacial lake surrounded by limestone cliffs. Families should definitely choose this trail because of how simple it is.

Pen-y-ghent Walk: This 6-kilometer hike is one of the most popular in the Yorkshire Dales. The trail climbs to the summit of Pen-y-ghent, one of the Three Peaks, offering panoramic views of the surrounding countryside.

Three Peaks Walk: This challenging 24-kilometer hike takes in the summits of Pen-y-ghent, Whernside, and Ingleborough, the Three Peaks of Yorkshire. The trail is not for the faint of heart, but the views from the top are worth it.

Whernside Walk: This 14-kilometer hike is the highest of the Three Peaks, with an elevation of 736 meters. The trail is not as challenging as the Three Peaks Walk, but it's still a great option for those looking for a challenging hike.

Ribblehead Viaduct Walk: This 8-kilometer hike takes you along the Ribblehead Viaduct, a 24-arch railway viaduct that spans the Ribble Valley. The trail is easy to follow and offers stunning views of the surrounding countryside.

These are just a few of the many hiking and walking trails in Yorkshire. There are trails to suit all levels of experience, so you're sure to find the perfect one for you.

In addition to these popular trails, there are also many lesser-known trails that are worth exploring. For example, the Studfold Adventure Trail is a great option for families with children. The trail is located in the Nidderdale Area of Outstanding Natural Beauty and features a variety of obstacles, including rope bridges, zip lines, and treehouses.

Another great option is the How Stean Gorge. This gorge is located in the Yorkshire Dales National Park and features a variety of hiking trails, as well as opportunities for rock climbing and caving.

You may locate the ideal hiking or walking trail in Yorkshire no matter what your interests are. So put your boots on and head out onto the trails!

8.2. Cycling Routes

Yorkshire is a cyclist's paradise(not only for hikers), with a wide variety of routes to choose from, ranging from easy family rides to challenging mountain bike trails. Here are a few of the best cycling routes in Yorkshire:

Wharfedale Cycleway: This 17-mile route follows the River Wharfe from Ilkley to Bolton Abbey, through some of the most beautiful scenery in Yorkshire. Since the route is largely flat, cyclists of various skill levels can ride it.

Nidderdale Way: This 50-mile route takes in some of the best of Nidderdale, including the stunning River Nidd, the dramatic Great Whernside, and the charming market town of Pateley Bridge. The route is challenging but rewarding, with plenty of hills to climb and stunning views to enjoy.

Rail Trail: This 18-mile route follows the old railway line between Skipton and Keighley, through some of the most picturesque countryside in Yorkshire. The route is mostly flat, making it ideal for families and less experienced cyclists.

Malham Tarn Circular: This 12-mile route takes in the stunning scenery around Malham Tarn, including the limestone pavements of Malham Cove and the spectacular Gordale Scar. The route is challenging but rewarding, with plenty of hills to climb and stunning views to enjoy.

Forest of Bowland Cycleway: This 30-mile route takes in some of the best of the Forest of Bowland, including the rolling hills, ancient woodlands, and charming villages. The route is challenging but rewarding, with plenty of hills to climb and stunning views to enjoy.

These are just a few of the many great cycling routes in Yorkshire. With so much to choose from, you're sure to find the perfect route for your next cycling adventure.

Other Cycling Activities in Yorkshire

In addition to road cycling, there are also a number of other cycling activities available in Yorkshire. These include:

Mountain biking: Yorkshire is home to some of the best mountain biking trails in the UK. There are trails to suit all levels of riders, from beginner to expert.

Gravel biking: Gravel biking is a relatively new form of cycling that is growing in popularity. Gravel bikes are designed to handle a variety of terrain, including roads, trails, and gravel paths.

Cyclocross: Cyclocross is a type of racing that takes place on a variety of terrain, including grass, mud, and gravel. Cyclocross races are typically short and intense, making them a great workout.

Bikepacking: Bikepacking is a form of cycling that involves carrying all of your gear with you on your bike. Bikepacking trips can be anything from a weekend overnighter to a multi-week expedition.

No matter what your level of experience or what type of cycling you enjoy, you're sure to find something to love in Yorkshire. With so many great cycling routes and activities to choose from, you're sure to have an unforgettable cycling adventure in Yorkshire.

Tips for Cycling in Yorkshire

Plan your route in advance. This will help you to choose a route that is suitable for your level of experience and fitness.

Check the weather forecast before you set off. Yorkshire can be a wet and windy place, so it's important to be prepared.

Wear appropriate clothing. This includes a helmet, sunglasses, and comfortable cycling shoes.

Bring plenty of water and snacks. It's important to stay hydrated and fueled when you're cycling.

Be aware of your surroundings. This includes other cyclists, pedestrians, and motorists.

Have fun! Cycling is a great way to explore Yorkshire and get some exercise.

8.3. Water Sports and Sailing

Yorkshire is a county with a long and rich history of water sports. From sailing on the placid waters of the Rivers Ouse and Wharfe to surfing on the wild waves of the North Sea, there is something for everyone here.

Sailing

Sailing is one of the most popular water sports in Yorkshire. There are many lakes and rivers in the county where you can sail, including the famous Lake Windermere. If you are a beginner, there are plenty of sailing schools in Yorkshire that offer lessons. Once you have mastered the basics, you can take your sailing to the next level by competing in one of the many regattas that are held throughout the year.

Some of the best places for sailing in Yorkshire include:

Lake Windermere
The River Ouse
The River Wharfe
The Humber Estuary
The North Sea

Surfing

Surfing is another popular water sport in Yorkshire. The best places for surfing in the county are along the coast, where the waves can be quite large. If you are a beginner, it is best to start surfing in the summer months, when the waves are smaller. Once you have mastered the basics, you can try surfing in the winter months, when the waves are bigger.

Some of the best places for surfing in Yorkshire include:

Bridlington
Scarborough
Filey
Cayton Bay
Staithes

Other Water Sports

In addition to sailing and surfing, there are many other water sports that you can enjoy in Yorkshire. These include:

Canoeing
Kayaking
Stand-up paddleboarding
Whitewater rafting
Jet skiing
Wakeboarding

Where to Go

There are many places where you can enjoy water sports in Yorkshire. Here are a few suggestions:

Bay Watersports: This company offers a variety of water sports activities, including sailing, windsurfing, canoeing, and kayaking. They are located in Bridlington, on the Yorkshire coast.

The Yorkshire Adventure Company: This company offers a variety of outdoor activities, including water sports. They are located in York, in the heart of Yorkshire.

Yorkshire Water: This company manages a number of lakes and rivers in Yorkshire, where you can enjoy water sports. They have a website with information about all of their sites.

When to Go

The best time to go water sports in Yorkshire depends on the type of water sport you want to do. For example, if you want to sail, the best time to go is during the summer months, when the weather is warm and the days are long. If you want to surf, the best time to go is during the winter months, when the waves are bigger.

How to Prepare

If you are planning on going water sports in Yorkshire, there are a few things you need to do to prepare. First, you need to make sure you have the right gear. This includes a swimsuit, a towel, sunscreen, and a hat. If you are going to be doing any water sports that require special equipment, such as sailing or surfing, you will need to rent or purchase that equipment.

Second, you need to check the weather forecast. Make sure the weather is going to be good for the type of water sport you want to do. If the weather is too windy or too rainy, you may not be able to go water sports.

Finally, you need to be aware of the risks involved in water sports. Water sports can be dangerous, so it is important to be careful. If you are not sure how to do a particular water sport, it is best to take a lesson from a qualified instructor.

Yorkshire is a great place to go water sports. There are many different water sports that you can enjoy, from the gentle paddling of canoeing to the exhilarating waves of surfing. With so many options to choose from, you are sure to find the perfect water sport for you.

8.4. Wildlife and Nature Reserves

Yorkshire is home to a wide variety of wildlife, from the iconic red squirrel to the rare black grouse. There are also many nature reserves and other protected areas where you can go to see these animals in their natural habitat.

Here are a few of the best wildlife and nature reserves in Yorkshire:

Ainsty Moor is a National Nature Reserve (NNR) in the heart of the Yorkshire Dales. It is home to a variety of wildlife, including red grouse, black grouse, curlew, golden eagle, and peregrine falcon. There are also many opportunities for walking, birdwatching, and photography.

Holme Fen is a National Nature Reserve in the East Riding of Yorkshire. It is one of the most important wetlands in the UK, and is home to a variety of wildlife, including water voles, otters, and dragonflies. There are also many opportunities for walking, birdwatching, and photography.

Yorkshire Wildlife Trust manages a network of nature reserves across Yorkshire. These reserves are home to a wide variety of wildlife, including badgers, foxes, deer, and many species of birds. There are also many opportunities for walking, birdwatching, and photography.

Ryedale Nature Park is a 400 square mile area of outstanding natural beauty in North Yorkshire. It is home to a variety of wildlife, including red squirrels, badgers, foxes, deer, and many species of birds. There are also many opportunities for walking, cycling, and horse riding.

Dales Millennium Forest is a 17,000 acre forest in the Yorkshire Dales. It is home to a variety of wildlife, including red squirrels, badgers, foxes, deer, and many species of birds. There are also many opportunities for walking, cycling, and horse riding.

These are just a few of the many wildlife and nature reserves in Yorkshire. With so much to see and do, you're sure to have a great time exploring the natural beauty of this county.

In addition to these nature reserves, there are also many other places where you can see wildlife in Yorkshire. For example, you can go birdwatching at one of the many RSPB reserves in the county, or you can go on a wildlife safari in the Yorkshire Dales.

No matter what your interests are, you're sure to find a wildlife experience to enjoy in Yorkshire. So get out there and explore!

Here are some additional tips for enjoying wildlife in Yorkshire:

Treat animals and their habitat with respect.
Stay on designated paths and trails.
Leave no trace.
Take your time and enjoy the experience.

With a little planning, you can have a safe and enjoyable wildlife experience in Yorkshire.

9. Immersing in Yorkshire's Culinary Delights

9.1. Traditional Yorkshire Dishes

From hearty pies and puddings to sweet treats and drinks, there's something for everyone to enjoy.

Here are 9 traditional Yorkshire dishes that you should try:

Yorkshire Pudding: This iconic dish is made with a batter of eggs, flour, and milk that is cooked in hot fat until it puffs up. Yorkshire puddings are traditionally served with roast beef, but they can also be enjoyed on their own.

Harrogate Tart: This tart is made with a flaky pastry crust filled with a rich mixture of eggs, cream, and cheese. Harrogate tarts are often served with a dollop of chutney or fruit compote.

Scotch Egg: This dish is made with a hard-boiled egg that is coated in sausage meat and breadcrumbs, then deep-fried. Scotch eggs are a popular pub snack, and they can also be served as part of a larger meal.

Yorkshire Curd Tart: This tart is made with a pastry crust filled with a creamy mixture of curd cheese, sugar, and eggs. Yorkshire curd tarts are often served with a dollop of clotted cream or custard.

Parkin: This dense cake is made with oats, treacle, spices, and dried fruits. Parkin is a traditional winter treat, and it is often served with a cup of tea.

Whitby Fishcakes: These fishcakes are made with a mixture of mashed potatoes, cod or haddock, and spices. Whitby fishcakes are often served with a tartar sauce or malt vinegar.

Smoky Apple and Black Pudding Pie: This pie is made with a pastry crust filled with a mixture of smoked apples, black pudding, and cheese. Smoky apple and black pudding pie is a hearty and flavorful dish that is perfect for a cold winter day.

Yorkshire Cheese Pie: This pie is made with a pastry crust filled with a mixture of cheese, eggs, and milk. Yorkshire cheese pie is a classic dish that is often served as part of a Sunday lunch.

Harrogate Black Pudding: This type of black pudding is made with pork blood, oats, spices, and suet. Harrogate black pudding is a regional specialty that is often served with a fried breakfast or as part of a larger meal.

These are just a few of the many traditional Yorkshire dishes that you can enjoy. Whether you're looking for a hearty meal or a sweet treat, there's sure to be something on this list that you'll love.

If you're looking for a truly authentic Yorkshire dining experience, be sure to check out some of the local restaurants and pubs. You'll find a wide variety of traditional dishes on the menu, and you're sure to leave feeling satisfied.

9.2. Local Breweries and Pubs

Yorkshire is awash with great beer, from traditional cask ales to modern craft brews. There are breweries to be found all over the county, from the bustling cities to the sleepy villages. And of course, no trip to Yorkshire would be complete without sampling a pint or two in one of the region's many famous pubs.

Here are 13 of the best local breweries and pubs in Yorkshire:

Black Sheep Brewery: This award-winning brewery is based in Masham, North Yorkshire. It's known for its hoppy ales, such as the White Witch and the Riggwelter.
Theakstons: Another Masham-based brewery, Theakstons is famous for its Old Peculier ale. It also produces a range of other beers, including the Landlord and the Jaipur.
Kirkstall Brewery: This brewery is located in Leeds. It's known for its range of modern craft beers, such as the Black Cat and the Pale Rider.

Saltaire Brewery: This brewery is based in Saltaire, West Yorkshire. It's known for its traditional cask ales, such as the Saltaire Best and the Saltaire Mild.

Brewdog: This Scottish brewery has a taproom in Leeds. It's known for its innovative craft beers, such as the Elvis Juice and the Punk IPA.

North Brewing Co: This brewery is based in Leeds. It's known for its range of hop-forward beers, such as the Northern Monk and the Persevere.

Stout & Co: This brewery is based in Sheffield. It's known for its range of stouts, porters, and other dark beers.

Maltsmiths: This brewery is based in Bradford. It's known for its range of traditional cask ales, such as the Bradford Bitter and the Bradford Gold.

Willow Tree Brewery: This brewery is based in Skipton, North Yorkshire. It's known for its range of farmhouse ales, such as the White Rabbit and the Black Cat.

Theakstons Old Original Brewery Tap: This pub is located in Masham, North Yorkshire. It's the only place in the world where you can sample Theakstons' Old Peculier on cask.

The Punch Bowl Inn: This pub is located in Ilkley, West Yorkshire. It's a popular spot for real ale lovers, and it has a wide selection of beers on tap.

The Golden Lion: This pub is located in York. It's a traditional Yorkshire pub with a warm and welcoming atmosphere.

The Three Tuns: This pub is located in Skipton, North Yorkshire. It's a historic pub with a charming interior.

These are just a few of the many great breweries and pubs in Yorkshire. With so much choice, you're sure to find something to your taste. So raise a glass and enjoy a pint of Yorkshire's finest beer!

Tips for Visiting Yorkshire's Breweries and Pubs:

If you're planning a trip to Yorkshire, be sure to check out the Yorkshire Beer Guide. It lists all of the breweries and pubs in the county, along with their contact information and opening hours.

Many breweries offer tours and tastings. This is a great way to learn about the brewing process and sample some of the brewery's beers.

If you're looking for a pub with a warm and welcoming atmosphere, be sure to check out one of the traditional Yorkshire pubs. These pubs are often family-owned and operated, and they have a great sense of community.

No visit to Yorkshire would be complete without sampling a pint of Yorkshire's finest beer. So raise a glass and enjoy!

9.3. Farmers' Markets and Food Festivals

From traditional Yorkshire puddings and fish and chips to more modern creations, there's something for everyone to enjoy.

One of the best ways to sample the best of Yorkshire's food is to visit one of the many farmers' markets or food festivals held throughout the year. These events offer a chance to meet local producers, sample their wares, and learn about the history and culture of Yorkshire's food.

Here are 11 of the best farmers' markets and food festivals in Yorkshire:

Harrogate Farmers' Market is one of the largest and most popular farmers' markets in Yorkshire. It's held every Saturday from 9am to 1pm in the town's Royal Baths Gardens.

Leeds Farmers' Market is another great option for those looking for a wide variety of local produce. It's held every Sunday from 9am to 1pm in Millennium Square.

York Farmers' Market is a great place to find traditional Yorkshire produce, such as Yorkshire puddings, Wensleydale cheese, and pork pies. It's held every Thursday from 9am to 2pm in St. Sampson's Square.

Whitby Farmers' Market is a charming market held in the historic town of Whitby. It's a great place to find fresh seafood, as well as other local produce. It's held every Saturday from 9am to 1pm in West Cliff Gardens.

Bradford Farmers' Market is a great place to find a diverse range of produce, from fresh fruits and vegetables to international cuisine. It's held every Sunday from 10am to 3pm in City Park.

Wakefield Farmers' Market is a great place to find local produce, as well as handmade crafts and gifts. It's held every Saturday from 9am to 1pm in Cathedral Square.

Doncaster Farmers' Market is a great place to find fresh produce, as well as street food and live music. It's held every Sunday from 9am to 1pm in Market Square.

Ryedale Food Festival is a large-scale food festival held in the town of Malton. It features over 150 exhibitors, as well as cookery demonstrations, live music, and children's activities. The festival is held every September.

Yorkshire Dales Food Festival is a celebration of the food and drink of the Yorkshire Dales. It features over 100 exhibitors, as well as cookery demonstrations, live music, and children's activities. The festival is held every July.

York Food and Drink Festival is a large-scale food festival held in the city of York. It features over 200 exhibitors, as well as cookery demonstrations, live music, and children's activities. The festival is held every October.

Harrogate International Food Festival is one of the largest food festivals in the UK. It features over 600 exhibitors, as well as cookery demonstrations, live music, and children's activities. The festival is held every November.

These are just a few of the many farmers' markets and food festivals held in Yorkshire throughout the year. So whether you're a foodie or just looking for a fun day out, be sure to check out one of these events. You won't be disappointed!

Other tips for enjoying Yorkshire's food:

Visit one of the many farm shops or restaurants that source their ingredients locally.

Take a cooking class and learn how to make traditional Yorkshire dishes.

Go on a food tour and sample the best of Yorkshire's cuisine.

Attend one of the many food festivals held throughout the year.

With so much delicious food to choose from, you're sure to enjoy your time in Yorkshire. So come on down and experience the culinary delights of this beautiful county!

10. Shopping in Yorkshire

10.1. Independent Boutiques and Shops

There are a number of independent boutiques and shops in Yorkshire that offer a unique and personal shopping experience. Here are 13 of the best:

The Great Northern Boutique in Leeds is a must-visit for anyone looking for high-end fashion. The boutique stocks a carefully curated selection of clothes, accessories, and homeware from some of the world's leading designers.

Stowford's in Harrogate is a family-run business that has been selling quality gifts and homeware for over 100 years. The store is full of unique and stylish items, and the staff are always happy to help you find the perfect gift.

The Yorkshire Shop in York is a great place to find traditional Yorkshire souvenirs and gifts.

The store stocks a wide range of products, including Yorkshire tea, Dales knitwear, and Whitby jet jewellery.

Redemption Vintage in Sheffield is a treasure trove of vintage clothing and accessories. The store is packed with unique pieces, and the prices are very reasonable.

The Hip Hop Shop in Leeds is a must-visit for any fan of hip hop culture. The store stocks a wide range of clothing, accessories, and music, and the staff are always happy to chat about the latest trends.

Kitsch & Knickknacks in Skipton is a great place to find quirky gifts and homeware. The store stocks a wide range of products, including vintage toys, retro posters, and unusual ornaments.

The White Rabbit in York is a unique boutique that stocks a carefully curated selection of clothes, accessories, and homeware. The store has a bohemian vibe, and the staff are always happy to help you find the perfect item.

The Art House in Ilkley is a great place to find unique and stylish gifts. The store stocks a wide range of products, including art prints, jewellery, and homeware.

The Mustard Shop in York is a must-visit for any fan of mustard. The store stocks over 100 different types of mustard, as well as a range of other condiments and chutneys.

The York Cocoa House in York is a great place to find handmade chocolate. The store stocks a wide range of chocolates, as well as chocolate-making kits and other chocolate-related products.

The Piping Pigeon in Settle is a great place to find traditional Yorkshire crafts. The store stocks a wide range of products, including hand-knitted jumpers, Dales pottery, and Whitby jet jewellery.

The Yorkshire Weaving Company in Settle is a great place to find traditional Yorkshire textiles. The store stocks a wide range of products, including hand-woven rugs, blankets, and scarves.

The Dales Countrystore in Hawes is a great place to find traditional Yorkshire produce. The store stocks a wide range of products, including

Yorkshire cheeses, Dales honey, and Wensleydale ales.

These are just a few of the many independent boutiques and shops in Yorkshire. With so many unique and stylish stores to choose from, you're sure to find something you love.

Tips for Shopping in Yorkshire

Visit the markets. Yorkshire is home to a number of great markets, where you can find everything from fresh produce to handmade crafts. Some of the best markets include the Kirkgate Market in Leeds, the Shambles Market in York, and the Skipton Farmers' Market.

Explore the independent shops. Yorkshire is full of independent shops, which offer a unique and personal shopping experience. Be sure to wander around the streets of your favorite town or city and see what you can find.

Support local businesses. When you shop at independent businesses, you're helping to support the local economy. This is especially important in Yorkshire, which is a rural county with a strong sense of community.

10.2. Antique and Vintage Stores

From the bustling markets of Leeds to the quaint shops of York, there are endless opportunities to find unique and special pieces.

Leeds

Leeds is a great place to start your antique and vintage shopping. The city has a number of well-established markets, including Kirkgate Market and Leeds Antiques Centre. Kirkgate Market is the largest covered market in Europe, and it's a great place to find everything from clothes and furniture to jewelry and toys. Leeds Antiques Centre is home to over 100 dealers, and it's a great place to find rare and unusual items.

If you're looking for something a little more unique, head to one of Leeds' many independent shops. Some of our favorites include:

The Vintage Twin: This shop specializes in 1950s and 1960s fashion, and it's a great place to find vintage dresses, skirts, and blouses.

The Antique Emporium: This shop is full of eclectic items, from furniture and jewelry to vintage posters and toys.

The Curiosity Shop: This shop is a great place to find unusual and hard-to-find items, such as vintage cameras, maps, and books.

York

York is another great city for antique and vintage shopping. The city has a number of long-standing shops, as well as a number of newer stores that have popped up in recent years.

Some of our favorite antique and vintage shops in York include:

The Shambles: This street is home to a number of antique shops, and it's a great place to wander and browse.

York Antiques Market: This market is held every Sunday, and it's a great place to find a wide variety of antiques and vintage items.

The Red Door: This shop specializes in vintage clothing, and it's a great place to find unique and stylish pieces.

The Vintage Warehouse: This shop is full of vintage furniture, homewares, and clothing.

Other Areas of Yorkshire

In addition to Leeds and York, there are a number of other areas in Yorkshire that are worth exploring for antique and vintage shopping. Some of our favorites include:

Harrogate: This town is known for its spas and its Georgian architecture, but it's also home to a number of great antique and vintage shops.

Scarborough: This seaside town is a great place to find vintage beachwear and other nautical-themed items.

Whitby: This historic town is home to a number of antique shops, as well as a number of shops that sell Whitby jet jewelry.

No matter where you go in Yorkshire, you're sure to find some great antique and vintage shops.

Tips for Antique and Vintage Shopping in Yorkshire

Be ready to haggle: In many circumstances, the cost of an antique or vintage item can be negotiated. Therefore, don't hesitate to negotiate a cheaper price.

Do your homework: Do some research on the products you're interested in before you start buying. Your understanding of fair pricing and what to look for will be aided by this.

Be persistent: Finding the ideal antique or vintage item requires patience. So if you don't immediately find what you're looking for, don't give up.

Have fun: Antique and vintage shopping is a great way to discover unique and special pieces.

So relax, enjoy the process, and see what you can find!

10.3. Artisan Crafts and Souvenirs

Yorkshire is a great place to find artisan crafts and souvenirs. Here are some of the most popular items to look for:

Yorkshire Pudding: This traditional Yorkshire dish is a must-have for any foodie. You can find Yorkshire puddings in all shapes and sizes, from small teacakes to large Yorkshires big enough to feed a family.

Yorkshire Tea: Yorkshire Tea is one of the most popular brands of tea in the UK. It's known for its strong, full-bodied flavor. You can find Yorkshire Tea in most supermarkets and souvenir shops.

Harrogate Rock: Harrogate Rock is a type of mineral that is found in the town of Harrogate. It's often carved into small figurines or other shapes. You can find Harrogate Rock in souvenir shops all over Yorkshire.

Saltaire Pottery: Saltaire Pottery is a type of pottery that is made in the village of Saltaire. It's known for its distinctive blue and white designs. You can find Saltaire Pottery in many shops in Saltaire, as well as in some souvenir shops in other parts of Yorkshire.

Whitby Jet: Whitby Jet is a type of fossilized wood that is found in the town of Whitby. It's often made into jewelry and other ornaments. You can find Whitby Jet in many shops in Whitby, as well as in some souvenir shops in other parts of Yorkshire.

Hebden Bridge Textiles: Hebden Bridge Textiles are a type of textiles that are made in the town of Hebden Bridge. They're known for their handmade, quality craftsmanship. You can find Hebden Bridge Textiles in many shops in Hebden Bridge, as well as in some souvenir shops in other parts of Yorkshire.

Here are some other places to find artisan crafts and souvenirs in Yorkshire:

The Piece Hall: The Piece Hall is a former cloth hall in Halifax that is now home to a variety of shops, including many that sell artisan crafts and souvenirs.

The Shambles: The Shambles is a historic street in York that is lined with shops, many of which sell traditional Yorkshire souvenirs.

Saltaire: Saltaire is a village in West Yorkshire that is known for its Victorian architecture and its Saltaire Pottery factory. There are many shops in Saltaire that sell artisan crafts and souvenirs.

Hebden Bridge: Hebden Bridge is a town in West Yorkshire that is known for its arts and crafts scene. There are many shops in Hebden Bridge that sell artisan crafts and souvenirs.

11. Insider Tips and Local Secrets

11.1. Hidden Gems and Lesser-known Attractions

Hackfall Woods in North Yorkshire is a picturesque woodland with secret waterfalls and hidden follies.

Staindrop is a charming village in the North York Moors National Park with a historic castle and a traditional market.

Heptonstall is a former mill town in the South Pennines with a dramatic setting and a number of historic buildings.

The Lost Summer House is a hidden folly in the Yorkshire Dales National Park that is only accessible by foot.

The World Famous Emett Machines in Leeds are a collection of miniature steam locomotives and other vehicles that were created by the artist Rowland Emett.

Barnsley Main Colliery is a former coal mine that has been preserved as a museum.

Lumb Hole Falls are a series of waterfalls in the Yorkshire Dales National Park.

Standedge Tunnel is a long-distance railway tunnel that passes through the Pennines.

Middleton Railway is a preserved railway that runs through the West Yorkshire countryside.

These are just a few of the many hidden gems and lesser-known attractions that Yorkshire has to offer. With its stunning scenery, rich history, and vibrant culture, Yorkshire is a region that is full of surprises.

Here are some additional tips for finding more hidden gems in Yorkshire:

Ask locals for recommendations.
Look for places that are off the beaten path.
Visit during the off-season.
Explore small villages and towns.
Look for places that have a unique history or character.

With a little bit of effort, you're sure to find some hidden gems in Yorkshire that will surprise and delight you.

11.2. Authentic Local Experiences

If you're looking for an authentic local experience in Yorkshire, here are a few ideas:

Visit a traditional market town. Yorkshire is home to some of the most beautiful market towns in the UK, such as Skipton, Ilkley, and Harrogate. These towns are full of character, with charming shops, cafes, and pubs.

Go on a walking tour. There are many great walking tours available in Yorkshire, which will take you to some of the most scenic spots in the county. You can learn about the history of the area, as well as see some of the local wildlife.

Visit a stately home. Yorkshire is home to some of the most impressive stately homes in the UK, such as Castle Howard, Harewood House, and Wentworth Woodhouse. These homes are open to the public, and you can take a tour to learn about their history and architecture.

Go on a steam train ride. Yorkshire is home to a number of steam train lines, which offer a unique way to see the countryside. You can ride on a steam train from York to Scarborough, or from Keighley to Oxenhope.

Visit a traditional Yorkshire pub. Yorkshire is famous for its traditional pubs, which are full of character and atmosphere. You can enjoy a pint of ale, a hearty meal, and some live music in a traditional Yorkshire pub.

Go for a hike in the Yorkshire Dales. The Yorkshire Dales are a UNESCO World Heritage Site, and they offer some of the most stunning scenery in the UK. You can go for a hike to one of the many waterfalls, or take a walk along one of the many rivers.

Visit a Yorkshire village. Yorkshire is home to many charming villages, such as Staithes, Robin Hood's Bay, and Whitby. These villages are full of character, and they offer a glimpse of traditional Yorkshire life.

These are just a few ideas for authentic local experiences in Yorkshire. With its rich history, its beautiful countryside, and its friendly locals, Yorkshire is a county that is sure to charm you.

Here are some additional tips for having an authentic local experience in Yorkshire:

Talk to the locals. The best way to learn about a place is to talk to the people who live there. Ask them about their favorite places to visit, their favorite things to do, and their favorite foods to eat.

Go off the beaten path. If you want to experience Yorkshire like a local, don't just stick to the tourist hotspots. Explore the smaller towns and villages, and get off the beaten path.

Try the local food. Yorkshire is home to some of the best food in the UK. Make sure to try some of the local favorites, such as Yorkshire pudding, fish and chips, and parkin.

Be respectful of the local culture. Yorkshire is a proud county with a rich history and culture. Be respectful of the local customs and traditions, and don't do anything that might be considered offensive.

12. Practical Information and Resources

12.1. Tourist Information Centers

Tourist Information Centers (TICs) are a great resource for travelers to Yorkshire. They could give you details about:

Places to visit
Things to do
Where to stay
Where to eat
How to get around
And more!

TICs are staffed by friendly and knowledgeable people who are happy to help you plan your trip. They can also provide you with maps, brochures, and other travel information.

There are TICs all over Yorkshire, so you're never far from one.

Here are some of the most popular TICs in Yorkshire:

York Visitor Centre: This TIC is located in the heart of York, just a short walk from York Minster. It's a great place to start your visit to York.

Harrogate Tourist Information Centre: This TIC is located in Harrogate, a beautiful spa town in North Yorkshire. It's a great place to find out about things to do in Harrogate and the surrounding area.

Leeds Visitor Centre: This TIC is located in Leeds, the largest city in Yorkshire. It's a great place to find out about things to do in Leeds and the surrounding area.

Whitby Tourist Information Centre: This TIC is located in Whitby, a charming seaside town in North Yorkshire. It's a great place to find out about things to do in Whitby and the surrounding area.

12.2. Emergency Contacts

Here are some emergency contacts that you may need while traveling in Yorkshire:

Police: 999
Fire: 999
Ambulance: 999
Coastguard: 999
Mountain Rescue: 999
NHS 111: 111
National Domestic Abuse Helpline: 0808 2000 247
Rape Crisis England: 0808 802 9999
Childline: 0800 1111

It is a good idea to have the emergency contact numbers for your country of origin saved on your phone, as well as the emergency contact numbers for Yorkshire. You can also add your emergency contacts to your phone's lock screen so that they can be accessed even if your phone is locked.

12.3. Health and Safety

Here are the health and safety tips for travelers to Yorkshire:

Be aware of the risk of flooding, especially in the winter months. If you are planning on visiting areas that are prone to flooding, check the weather forecast before you travel and be prepared to change your plans if necessary.

Check the weather forecast before you travel and dress appropriately. Yorkshire can experience a wide range of weather conditions, so it is important to be prepared for anything. In the summer, it can be hot and sunny, but in the winter, it can be cold and wet.

Be aware of the risk of ticks, especially in the countryside. Ticks can carry Lyme disease, so it is important to take precautions if you are going to be spending time in wooded areas. Put on long sleeves, long pants, and socks that are tucked into your pant legs. Regularly check yourself for ticks, and if you do, gently remove it before consulting a doctor.

Drink lots of fluids, especially if you're exercising vigorously or going on a hike. It's crucial to drink enough of water because Yorkshire may get very hot and dry. Avoid sugary beverages, and drink lots of water.

Be aware of the risk of sunburn, especially in the summer months. The sun can be very strong in Yorkshire, so it is important to protect your skin. Wear sunscreen with an SPF of at least 30, and reapply it regularly.

If you are feeling unwell, seek medical attention as soon as possible. There are a number of good hospitals and clinics in Yorkshire, so you should be able to get the care you need.

12.4. Useful Websites and Apps

Google Maps is a digital mapping application that was created by the search engine giant. It provides real-time traffic information, street maps, 360-degree panoramic views, street view, and satellite data.

Visit Yorkshire: The official tourism website for Yorkshire, with information on all the region's attractions, events, and places to stay.

Yorkshire Dales National Park: Website of the Yorkshire Dales National Park, with information on hiking, camping, and other outdoor activities.

North Yorkshire Moors National Park: Website of the North Yorkshire Moors National Park, with information on hiking, biking, and other outdoor activities.

Yorkshire Waterways: Website of Yorkshire Waterways, with information on boat trips, canal walks, and other water-based activities.

TransPennine Express: Website of TransPennine Express, the train operator that serves Yorkshire.

National Rail Enquiries: Website for planning train journeys in the UK.

Citymapper: App for planning public transport journeys in cities around the world, including Leeds, Sheffield, and York.

What3Words: App for finding and sharing locations using a unique three-word address.

TripAdvisor: Website and app for finding and booking accommodation, restaurants, and activities.

Yelp: Website and app for finding and booking accommodation, restaurants, and activities.

13. Conclusion: Making the Most of Your Yorkshire Adventure

13.1. Reflecting on Your Journey

As your remarkable Yorkshire adventure draws to a close, take a moment to reflect on the incredible experiences you've had, the sights you've seen, and the emotions that have touched your heart. Yorkshire has a way of leaving a lasting imprint on the souls of its visitors, and now is the time to cherish those memories.

Think back to the awe-inspiring vistas of the Yorkshire Dales, the whispers of history in the ancient streets of York, and the warm embrace of the local community. Let the essence of Yorkshire linger within you, reminding you of the beauty that exists in the world and the extraordinary moments that make life truly meaningful.

13.2. Creating Lasting Memories

As you bid farewell to this captivating county, remember that the memories you've created here will stay with you forever. Capture the magic of Yorkshire in photographs, write down your most cherished moments, and share your stories with friends and loved ones. Let your experiences inspire others to embark on their own journeys of discovery.

13.3. Farewell to Yorkshire

As we conclude this travel guide, we extend our heartfelt gratitude for allowing us to be a part of your Yorkshire adventure. We hope that our insights, tips, and recommendations have enriched your trip and helped you create unforgettable memories. Farewell to Yorkshire, but never farewell to the spirit of discovery and the joy of exploration that it has awakened within you.

Remember, Yorkshire will always welcome you back with open arms, ready to share new secrets and unveil hidden treasures. May your journeys continue to be filled with wonder, and may the memories of your Yorkshire adventure forever brighten your path. Safe travels, and may your love for exploration never fade.